LOVE SEEKER

Part Three

Recovered

Barbara Ann Quinlan

Copyright © Barbara Ann Quinlan, 2021
Published: 2021 by The Book Reality Experience

ISBN: 978-0-6489497-8-7 Paperback Edition
ISBN: 978-0-6489497-9-4 EBook Edition

All rights reserved.

The right of Barbara Ann Quinlan to be identified as the author of this Work has been asserted by her in accordance with sections 77 and 78 of the Copyright, Designs and Patents Act 1988.

This book is a memoir, reflecting the author's present recollections of experiences over time. This means that some details may vary from fact. Some names and characteristics have been changed, some events have been compressed, and some dialogue has been recreated. Memory can be a fickle thing, so the Author trusts that any minor errors in times, dates and details of particular events will be understood.

Some names and identifying details have been changed to protect the privacy of individuals.

No part of this publication may be reproduced, stored in a retrieval system, copied in any form or by any means, electronic, mechanical, photocopying, recording or otherwise transmitted without written permission from the publisher.

Front Cover Photo: The Author
Cover Design by Luke Buxton | www.lukebuxton.com

To my beloved daughter Raphael,
who rescued me.

Author's Note

This book is a memoir and as the dictionary will tell you, a memoir is a historical account or biography written from personal knowledge. This memoir is my memoir and so is written with and from my personal knowledge. Where that differs from the historical record, as decided on, or written, by others, then I can only say, that's not how I recall it.

Where it differs from your own knowledge, should you be in or near to my life, or the situations I describe, then again, I can but say, we see from our own eyes.

Being my present recollections of experiences, tempered by the passing of time, I have no doubt that some details may vary from supposed fact. Some names and characteristics may have been changed, some events compressed, and some dialogue recreated. All I can offer is that despite memory being fickle, I have told no lies, nor included any statements that I believe to be untrue. I offer no hurt, nor malice.

I am and always have been a seeker of Love and so I only offer that within these pages. That you may read them and love them for what they are. A story.

My story.

Barbara
New York City
2021

Chapter Fifteen – Zohar 2

My sister, Kate was waiting for me in Forest Lake, Minnesota. I was to go and stay with her for a month to help research a book she was writing about child abuse. Kate was a social worker turned supervisor at Social Services in Hennepin County and had recently won a national award for her adolescent parent program.

She lived with her husband and two children in a lovely Tudor-style home on the edge of a pond complete with snapping turtles.

In the music room there was a Steinway upright, which she had not played since our parents had visited the year before. She told me she had practiced for months before their arrival. When she finally sat Dad down to hear her play again, he wept and told her, "I did not know you could still play like that!"

To me, it was as if she had built a perfectly normal life. As an idealist, she had a strong belief that she could make a difference in the world and her passion at that time was a war against child abuse.

I was touched by Kate's kindness and confidence in me. Every morning I went with her to work. I would head to the law library to spend the day researching for her except for the time we would meet for lunch. One thing in particular stands out after 20 days pawing through research and Kate's own files; men rarely get over sexual abuse in childhood. The theory is that men will not talk about it, share it, or cry over it as women tend to do. Yet when I opened up to Kate about my experience with our father, she froze and told me, "I don't want to talk about this!"

It was years later when she told me about her own encounter with our father. How did we all find one another? Or is it that there are just so many of us?

I called Beatrice one morning while still in Minnesota as Pini and she had finally decided to marry and I wanted to find out if her wedding plans had been finalized. The fact that she was now six months pregnant may have factored into that decision. I had spoken with Rabbi Kelemer about their situation, being that Pini was a Cohen and by Halakah (Jewish law) was forbidden to marry a convert. An Orthodox rabbi could marry a convert, but a Cohen cannot without surrendering his priestly stature. Cohen is the highest level of the Jewish caste system.

Rabbi Kelemer, like many rabbis, was a very practical man. I explained to him that they had been living together already for ten years and that she was now quite pregnant. He said then it is fait accompli. So he did take Beatrice on as a student, and she was ready to convert. However, this day on the phone she would coldly tell me in her most exasperated southern tone of voice that Rabbi Katz, the only Orthodox rabbi whose conversions were accepted in Israel, was refusing to perform the conversion. He had found out she was planning to marry a Cohen. I was outraged and told her to hang on while I call Rabbi Kelemer.

"Never mind," she said. "Just leave it be."

"Wait!" I told her and hung up.

I called Rabbi Kelemer immediately. Unfortunately, he verified the story Bea told me that Rabbi Katz did not want to be involved in such a questionable conversion. I apologized to Rabbi Kelemer for my part in what had most likely gotten him in trouble. He was kindly more concerned about the disappointment he knew Beatrice and Pini must have been suffering.

I told him, "Okay, just give me a few minutes to see if I can figure this out. I'll call you back!"

I put the phone down and started pacing the floor back-and-forth, like an actor holding a script that he was memorizing. I am a good study and I have an extraordinary memory. I let my brain search through everything I knew about Jewish law, and then it hit me!

I dialed back Kelemer's number as fast as I could, and when he answered I told him, "Call Rabbi Katz and tell him he must do the conversion because of the supreme law that says when a human life is at stake, all other laws are set aside! She is six months pregnant. If he refuses to perform this conversion, she could have a hysterical miscarriage, risking both her life and that of the child!" I was right, there was no question about it.

Rabbi Kelemer agreed, obviously relieved and proud of me, as his student.

The wedding would take place at the home of their friends in Bel-Air before the week's end. Kate and I agreed it was time for me to leave. I like to think the research I did there was of some help to her.

I arrived at the wedding house in a gorgeous cream-colored designer suit with a cigarette skirt and a plunging collared jacket. In my pocket was a light green compact-sized container filled with cocaine for my personal use. I did look chic despite the fact that I had already been up for at least 24 hours doing blow.

I was quickly shuffled up to the master suite where I found Beatrice gazing in the vanity mirror. Her wedding gown ported a poncho-like, draping over her baby bulge. The venue was beautiful, with round tables to accommodate 250 people set around the swimming pool, and the chuppah was overlooking the city. If, as Pini and Beatrice stood beneath it about to take their vows, Pini turned around to the crowd explaining that he changed his mind, the applause would have been deafening. Despite having had great difficulty finding a rabbi who would perform the ceremony, here they were, taking their vows.

Pini entertained at his own wedding and though several other Israeli singers had come to join him, Zohar was not among them. Rabbi Kelemer was there, and we danced the hora onstage together. As we were returning to our seats, several women who hated me as much as they did Bea approached the rabbi in front of me. "Did you know she is a follower of a Teacher?"

Rabbi Kelemer turned calmly to me and asked, "To whom are you grateful for the gift of this life, your Teacher or Hashem (God)?"

"God, of course!" I replied. "I owe my life to the creator. The gift that allowed me a deeper appreciation of this life was from my Teacher."

Kelemer turned back to the women and said, "You see? She knows!" I am fairly certain those ladies had no idea what I knew, but the fact that the rabbi would not join them in denouncing me made an impression nonetheless.

When I left the party, I went back to my apartment in

Beachwood Canyon, dropped my bags on the floor, and sat silently for several moments. I was up for at least another day doing coke, line after line. I had just returned from so many holy days in Israel. When I was at Zohar's side, I needed nothing more. My love for him was intoxicating. My devotion to love itself was unwavering. But as soon as we were apart, I tore myself apart.

I loved Zohar with all my heart and soul, and now I was away from him, at least in the physical sense. We would never really be separated; nothing, not even death would ever separate us. Our souls were eternally entwined. Yet, what was it that allowed me, even forced me, to leave? Was it only because I could not bear to watch Zohar destroy himself? Was it the force of destiny that kept pushing me onward? Or was it that I was cowardly in the face of a love that demanded everything?

Now as I sat alone in my room, the pain of separation that the illusion of distance brings was unbearable, and I sought to quell it. If, as some say, my lover is my mirror, what here and now would I see of myself reflecting back to me? Only upon reflection does the possible lesson plan show itself, giving me courage and urging me to tell the rest.

I too loved what was bad and was often tempted to push the limits of survival, seeking the sensuous rush that came with the next hit. I had always been so judgmental of junkies and was free to live in the sanctuary of the sanctified but I chose to dally down another road.

As I strove to start working in any aspect of the film industry, I was on 48-hour coke jags at least twice a month. I noticed that I was likely to accept a midnight coke invitation just before my period or when ovulating. I figured that was when my resistance was at its lowest and my passions were at their highest! I would get a call, usually late in the night, from Roni and Marin, who would already have been basing for a while. I'd go over, telling myself I'd just go to do a few hits and be back by 2 or 2:30 am. But it would never be like that. I was always there until at least dawn or the dawn after that.

Once, when Roni first started shooting cocaine, there was a beautiful, intelligent young woman with him, her long dark brown hair fell in straight sheets over her thin shoulders. For whatever personal reasons or private cause, she was laying her body down for cocaine. Roni had called me over. Whatever he was hoping for there was no way I could be convinced to have sex with this young woman for his entertainment. I saw her as a human being and was touched by her plight. I spoke openly with her about the gift, changing the atmosphere to something bright and hopeful, as much as could be between the periodic rushes of cocaine running up our veins.

It must be a miracle that none of us ever got Hep C. Roni was extremely careful about cleaning the needles, and thankfully, it wasn't long before he rejected that means of self-abuse. I left the two of them alone together there, handing her my phone number as I walked out the door.

A few months later she called me and asked if I'd like to join her at a party. It was near my house in the canyon, so I said sure I'll come by for a bit. When I arrived, it was only her and three men in suits standing around, all snorting cocaine while she filled her syringe. I was never quite sure if she had called me to join her or rescue her. But despite the fact that I was attracted to her and even to the situation, I did not believe I could afford to live with the possible consequences of such a night. I apologized sincerely for leaving her and I never saw her again. I do not know what became of her. I only hope she found her way back to dignity.

By now Marin had left her husband and was living with Roni. She felt guilty about leaving her marriage and took nothing with her but the clothes on her back. She didn't sue him for alimony. She didn't demand that he sell the house. She just left, taking a single apartment for herself on her first step out, although she almost never stayed there. Perhaps she took it to soften the blow that she was leaving him for someone else.

Roni, once a successful hairdresser with his own shop, was now a cocaine junkie and dealer. The Israeli mafia in Los Angeles was in its heyday, and Roni was one of its lesser kingpins. He and Marin changed residences at least once a year. Likely after an extended period of cocaine-induced paranoia, they would become suspicious of their neighbors and slip away to somewhere else.

There are memories locked up with each of their abodes, like their apartment on Kings Road where we had spent days and nights smoking cocaine together. We would all sit together on Roni's king-size bed passing the pipe and talking as if we knew what the universe was, thinking we were geniuses spurred on by the rising dopamine levels. And often Marin and I would talk to Roni about the gift.

Marin received the gift fresh out of high school with two girlfriends who are sisters. She was clearheaded about it, and until now had practiced every day. Neither of us could deny that we knew the difference between truth and illusion, but how often we chose to linger in the illusion! Some of the sensations that came with the chemical rush would remind us of the beauty of our breath. Then we remembered that we had the gift and we would speak of it.

Roni would remain fascinated for a while by the tone and the tenderness of the turn in conversation. Then something would jar his nerves, perhaps the last hit he took didn't quite set. I have never seen anything bring out selfishness more than a plate of cocaine, be it rock or powder.

There were many times Roni seriously misjudged me. It was probably Patty who spread the rumor that I was a martial artist. Roni was always curious to see what I could do, but I refused to show him. One afternoon he started to attack Marin in front of me. I pulled him away from her and then he came after me. I held off striking him as long as I possibly could, until he struck my forehead with stiffened fingers, cutting open my skin. Only then did I strike him with the back of my closed fist, so fast that he never even saw it coming. The force of the strike against his jaw was such that the bridge a dentist had recently cemented in popped out and was sitting on his tongue!

Roni cried out and looked at me in complete shock. The fight ended at that moment. He tried to demand that I leave immediately, but Marin interceded saying, "You can't let her go looking like this!" Blood was dripping down my face. Unbelievably enough, I stayed with them many more hours. I washed up the blood, put a little alcohol on it, and used Scotch tape to seal it back together. Then I sat down and tortured myself for several more hours.

Roni would get me back one day. Part of the cocaine game is who falls asleep first. No matter how much stuff you have access to, eventually you have to stop or die. Usually in the process of trying to mellow out, one drinks or drugs themselves with downers into a stupor and falls asleep, often holding the glass pipe in their hand.

On one such night Roni fell asleep after possibly a week of smoking. Marin and I were just sitting there aching badly for more but too paranoid to make a single move for fear he would wake up.

Finally, I couldn't take it anymore and dared to reach for the coke to see if she and I could get another hit. The fact that he woke right away makes me wonder now if Marin didn't shake his leg or something to wake him. He sucker-punched me in the mouth and just as quickly grabbed a gun that I'd never seen before. He waved the gun at both of us, screaming hysterically. His face was full of hate, and his eyes were that of a madman. Marin begged him to let me go. He ordered me out of the room but wouldn't let me take anything with me, even my purse.

I left the apartment immediately and went looking for help. The one person I knew in the building saw my lip bleeding through the peephole and refused to let me in. The next thing I heard was a police siren. I continued down the corridor and out the back exit, where I hid in the backyard shrubbery for what seemed like forever, terrified but determined not to get caught. I waited until the lights stopped flashing and the coast was clear. Then I went back to get my purse.

When I entered the apartment, I found they had taken Roni on a gun charge but left Marin there. She wanted to get out of there and asked if she could come with me. I said sure, and we called a taxi. Sitting in the back of the cab I opened my purse to get my wallet out. I was totally shocked to find that Roni had put half a kilo in my purse, knowing the police were on their way and figuring if they found it, he could say it was mine!

When Marin and I arrived at my place we were totally shook up. No sooner had we started drawing out some lines on the glass coffee table when there was a furious knock at the door. On instinct, I scooped out about an ounce and tucked it away. Then I took the rest and hid that before answering the door.

It turned out to be one of Roni's gangster friends, who had come looking for his stuff. Roni must've called him from the jail and told him in Hebrew what to do. Imagine blowing his one phone call to save the coke! I handed him the large packet, and he asked me if that's all there was. I told him yes, and walked him out the door.

***

Meanwhile, Zohar was going through his own hell. As an entertainer of his caliber it was not possible for a lost weekend to go by unnoticed by the world around him. There were 4,000 people waiting for him at a television station in Jerusalem, and he did not show up! Too stoned, no doubt.

Another time his manager put him into a cab, paid the driver in cash, and told him, "Don't let him out of the car until you get to Jerusalem!"

But Zohar had made other plans. Halfway there, he told the driver he had to pee and instructed him to pull over to the side of the road by a billboard so he could relieve himself behind it.

Zohar stood behind the billboard 15 minutes or so until he finally returned to the cab with pipe, crack, and torch in hand. It was 5 am when he finally stumbled up onto the stage eating a boureka (puff pastry with filling), and there were still 700 people sitting there waiting for him! Was that love? All the admiration in the world would not help him. I wonder now if his audiences somehow knew that their chances to see him were growing short.

He was standing on the stage singing when Sioni, the owner of a famous nightclub at the beach, noticed Zohar was swaying uncharacteristically. More and more often Zohar was getting stoned before going onstage. "Getting stoned" for him now meant basing as well as chasing the dragon (smoking opium).

After Zohar's performance, Sioni sat him down for dinner and a talk. Zohar looked at the wonderful spread of food set out before him and remarked, "You know, only here we celebrate over food. Everywhere else they give me drugs."

Sioni looked at his friend heavyhearted, then taking a deep breath said, "Zohar. Let me help you get off this shit. Come with me to Eilat, we'll put you in a hotel room, I'll hire some doctors, you'll have everything you need to quit if you want!" Zohar was so deeply touched by his friend's concern and was silent though for an instant it almost seemed that he might cry, "Okay. I want!"

Sioni patted Zohar's back. This would be the first of many times that he would go through the hell of attempting to quit opium cold turkey. The cocaine withdrawal brought with it a more psychological torture, but withdrawing from opium brought a physical agony that wracked his body with pain. Once Zohar had agreed to the process, guards were placed at the door, and doctors intermittently checked in on him.

It was all said and done, when my phone rang one afternoon. By luck and grace, I was there to answer. It was

Zohar! What mirrors we were for one another, and only now do I see it! The sole difference was that I knew where home was and how to get there. Perhaps Zohar kept hoping if he brought me back to his side in Israel one day he could find his way home too!

"Zohar! Mah shelom hah?" ("How are you?")

"Beseder. Mah shelomekh?" ("Okay. How are you?")

"Ani, Baruch Ha-Shem" ("I am, thank God.") "I just finished another screenplay!"

"So you write the truth?"

"Yes, I write the truth."

"You want to come back home?"

"Yes," I said.

"So come."

***

At last I would return to Israel, to my love and my life, on a break from binges. I boarded El-Al in an Yves St. Laurent suit, with a gold silk shirt buttoned up to the neck. My bags were misplaced, and it was 48 hours before they arrived at Zohar's new penthouse in Givatayim. The living room had no furniture. My bedroom was a mattress made up as a bed on the floor. Zohar's room was in the loft up a steel spiral staircase. He had a bed and a nightstand. The kitchen was equipped enough for Ema (Mother) to come and cook on occasion.

I had arrived in time for Pesach (Passover). One of Zohar's brothers met me at his penthouse with orders to bring me immediately to Ema's for the feast. I had no clothes to change into or time to take a bath, so I kept splashing an intense Henri Monet perfume on me, without realizing it would overwhelm the taste of the food. Zohar wouldn't mention it to me until the next day when he gently suggested that in the future, rac tippah ("only a little bit"), as he mimed dabbing on perfume.

When I arrived at Yona's, I found Zohar cooking cocaine in her kitchen. I was shocked to see how far Zohar's addiction had become. "Go from here!" he barked.

I obeyed and went into the large room to help his mother and sisters finish setting the Seder table. Long after the time for Seder to begin had passed, I ventured back into the kitchen. "Zohar please, we are all hungry. If you cannot leave this, (indicating the pipe), bring it to the table with you!"

"It's not me! It's Jacob we're waiting for!"

Jacob, ah yes, the older brother, his father's first son from his first wife. Just then Jacob arrived, and we all gathered in the large dining room, Zohar with pipe in hand. Watching him smoke cocaine evoked no desire for it in me as it did in L.A. where the attraction was so strong. Here I enjoyed the high of love itself that emanated from within me, and the plumes of smoke were no more than benign vapors.

Now with all the family seated around the table, Seder began. Zohar was the first to read, and when he had finished the opening section of the Haggadah, he handed the book to me. There was a skeptical murmur among the family members when I stood to read in English. As my voice infused meaning into each word there was complete silence. When I finished reading, the applause was spontaneous. Surprised and somewhat embarrassed, I sat and handed the book to the next reader.

Zohar turned to me and said, "God gave you too much power. I will take some from you!"

Later that night we returned to the new penthouse, and I retired to my own room. In the morning I climbed up the spiral staircase to the master bedroom, checking to see if I could get anything for Zohar. I sat down gently beside him.

Zohar studied my face for a moment as if looking into a mirror. "You know everyone think ani criminaly."

"You're not a criminal; you're an artist. People don't understand what it is to be an artist. You go up; you go down."

Zohar smiled and pointed to the new scar on his chin, "You see this? Now I am Scarface."

"What happened?"

"An accident, car accident."

"On the road to the beach at Rishon?"

Zohar was stunned by my uncanny question. "How do you know that?"

"I saw it happen once when we were on that road."

"You see! That is why I cannot marry you. You Rabbi, ani Rabbi. You should go and be Rabbanit!"

"But I love you!"

"Stop to love me!"

I got up and started to leave his room, then turning back at the top of the spiral staircase I told him, "If you don't care about me, care about the others. The people love you, they depend on you, and if you continue to go down, you will take them all with you!"

One lovely afternoon, drinking coffee in Yona's front room, Zohar placed a small cassette player on the table in front of us. Holding a cassette in his hand, he began, "I have to record one more song for the last cassette. I do with Asher, then we're finished. You will come when I make the record."

"Okay."

Then, almost shyly, he added, "I have something for you. It's a song called 'Yasmine'. I'm sorry I couldn't write it myself, but I sing it for you, and I put it on the cassette for you!"

I was speechless as Zohar put the cassette into the player.

"There are two recordings of it here. I want you to listen and tell me which is best, and I put that one on the album."

We sat together listening to the sweet romantic song. Tears streamed down my cheeks as Zohar smiled at me. His face was full of pride. He could see that he had made me very happy. I wiped the tears from my face as the song ended.

"Thank you. I love it!"

We arrived late to the recording studio. Asher and the technicians had almost given up waiting for him when I walked through the door quickly followed by Zohar, who entered carrying a base pipe and went directly into the sound booth with it. Asher slapped himself on the forehead, shaking his head.

Zohar soon appeared, standing behind the microphone, ready to work.

"I sing, she dance. She don't dance, I don't sing."

I stood in front of the glass where Zohar could see me and danced for him quite seductively as he began to sing. Asher was about to lose his mind.

"Please, this is a crazy man. Sit down!"

I did sit down, against Zohar's bemused protest.

Some days or weeks later, I was back in my room packing again when Zohar walked in. He crossed over to a picture of my father, picked it up, kissed him, and set the picture back in its place. Then he walked out of the room without a word. Before leaving I went up the spiral staircase to see him.

"Zohar, you remember when you told me 'stop to love me'? I love you more! Ani oheveet ota, layolam!!" ("I will love you forever!!")

"At ladat mah ze, layolam?"

"Yes, forever!"

Zohar smiled and wrapped his arms around me.

***

Not long after my return, my father's Parkinson's took a turn for the worse. When he was 65 years old, he could still press a handstand on the living room floor and flip over, landing on his feet, with my mother screaming in the background, "Jack, you're going to kill yourself. You'll have a heart attack!"

Two years later he was diagnosed with Parkinson's. The sentence and the symptoms had never sat well with him. The loss of physical control was devastating for him. By the time he was 72, the disease was out of control. One morning my mother called to tell me that he was shaking so violently he shook himself out of bed. I dropped whatever I was doing and went to see him immediately. When I entered the house, he was sitting in the kitchen. I greeted him warmly, sat down, and held his hands for a moment. I poured my energy into him. Then I stood up behind him, placed my hands on his shoulders, and again I let my energy pour through him. All the trembling stopped. Never again did he shake so violently. But sometimes a disease turns from its yang version into its yin counterpart, as in his case, when the tremors stopped the delirium began.

I saw him the night before he died. He had been taken to the hospital with symptoms of pneumonia. I brought him his favorite flower, the bird of paradise. He begged me to take him home. I explained that only Mother had the authority to do that, as she stood nearby. Then he asked me for a cigarette. Of course, as he was lying in a hospital bed, I couldn't give him one. I could've demanded that they put him in a wheelchair and wheel him outside, but I didn't. Every dying man should have a smoke if he wants it. I have never forgiven myself for not giving it to him!

That same day my brother John had checked into rehab for alcoholism. It was the day before John's birthday, and I was going to visit him afterwards. I told my father I loved him over and over again before leaving, explaining that I needed to go give John a cake but that I didn't really want to leave him. He told me, "Go, take care of John. I love you!"

It was after midnight when I returned home, and I was only there a few minutes when the phone rang. It was Mother. Dad was dead. An overwhelming sense of peace came over me. He was finally free from the bondage of disease.

I remember reading that Aristotle said that in death, one could not be truly happy until they could see that their children and grandchildren were also happy. When I was a teenager, who could barely see beyond herself, that seemed utterly ridiculous to me. Yet this idea continues to surface in mythology, and now it actually made some sense to me. I felt for a few moments that he was near me, wanting to comfort me and beckoning me to be a good girl for him. Then I called Roni.

Roni took pity on me and said I could come over right away. Marin and he had not started smoking yet, but he ordered some when he knew I was on my way. It was probably just an excuse to get high.

I stayed with them for 48 hours straight, no sleep, and then drove out to see my mother, an hour down the freeway! It was much like that night peaking on mescaline yet finding Spark's place in Claremont. I truly don't know how I managed to get there in one piece. I only know that it was as if the car was being driven by some other force, and I remember thinking I heard angels singing in the rustling bushes that lined the freeway. I knew I was way too high to be driving, but I prayed and pressed on!

When Mother opened the door, I had never seen her look so old. Clearly the sorrow of my father's death had taken its toll on her, and she must have been worried sick about me. My uncle Bill Shuster, commonly known as Broadway Bill in the baseball world, would shake his finger at me later saying, "Hey, next time call your mother!"

In the morning, I went to the funeral home to see Dad lying in a coffin looking like an empty milk carton. I felt no recrimination from him for my delay in arriving. As I stood gazing at his corpse, I suddenly felt a mass of energy undulating next to me, as if breathing. I knew it was him. It was clear that he was trying to tell me that this life is eternal, that he was still there.

If energy can neither be created nor destroyed, does it carry with it the consciousness? I could almost hear him talking to me, telling me to lead a good life. As I was leaving, I told him again I loved him. Then I heard him say, "Close the lid."

Ah yes, that would be Jack's request. Having been gorgeous all his life, he most definitely did not want to be seen dead, the least attractive look. I walked back beside him and looking in said, "You know Mother would kill me."

Again, I disrespected a simple request of his. However, that night after the Rosary, my oldest brother would come up to me weeping and said, "Please, close the coffin for me? I can't bear to do it!"

And so I did.

The next day at the gravesite, the same priest who had presided over the Rosary the night before and Mass that morning, now stood with the family waiting to say the final prayers. I had not appreciated the manner in which he said the Rosary the night before, and he had continued with his banal delivery throughout the Mass. If you're going to bother to say a prayer, let it mean something. Something else about him was annoying me. He did not have the priestly pallor I once found so appealing. I raised my hand to him in a full stop as he approached the coffin that would soon be lowered into the ground. He got the message and stepped backed immediately. I opened the Bible I was carrying to the 23rd Psalm and read it aloud. Then I closed the book and walked away. Two years later, that priest's arrest for child molestation made network news.

The man I loved was far away, and in the vacuum, I continued an attempt to construct my life. I started in the film industry by creating spectacular craft services, easy for a foodie and excellent hostess. My work showed such competency that I was soon moved up to the position of production assistant. I worked very well with others because I knew how to be what they wanted me to be and how they wanted to be treated.

I continued to maintain my privacy. I was careful not to let anyone even know that I smoked cigarettes, let alone my other drug habits. The shame I felt regarding the addiction was so intense that I would leave the set and walk down the alley between several buildings until I could finally find a place where I could smoke a cigarette unseen.

The work was always sporadic, so there was plenty of time in between to get high, and as almost all of my friends were doing cocaine in some form or another, hanging out with them often involved doing a line or two. That was all it would take to get me longing and looking for more. Usually I'd wind up at Roni's or Jack's, who was now basing cocaine as well. My company seemed welcome, especially while getting high. I almost never had to buy it; it was just there everywhere. I did, however, become an expert at stealing it, and sometimes the money to buy it. It was always darkly amusing to me that I would've made a great cat burglar.

There was a nice couple in Beachwood Canyon that I had bought from on occasion. I called them before dawn one morning to see if I could come by and get something. The husband kindly explained that they were asleep and asked me to call later. Instead I went over to their house at the break of dawn. I can't imagine what I was expecting to do, but when I got there, I discovered their kitchen window was open. I climbed through it. When I had bought something there before, he had gone into the kitchen and returned with the stuff. So I knew I was in the right room. I knew also that they were sleeping as I stood in their house.

Thanks to my work with Ossetynski, not only was I able to enter and leave without ever being heard, but I had this peculiar ability to lock onto an object and find it rather quickly. I opened the drawer at the desk and in the very back I found the bottled grams I was looking for. I took several and left just as quietly as I had entered. The intensity of the adrenalin rush that comes with executing such a feat has a high in and of itself. But they were such nice people. I was a little ashamed to take it from them.

Still, it did not stop me from repeating the same thing one more time a few weeks later. This time, however, I was seen climbing out the window by someone who was able to give a description of me. There was a phone call questioning whether or not I might know who it was. Of course, I never confessed, but I never went back either.

One night when I was smoking with Roni and Marin, Roni asked me to take something over to Gingi. He was the friend that Roni and I had ridden horses with so many times. I had no reason to fear him. I could not imagine he would ever do me any harm. I had always suspected that he was attracted to me but there was nothing unusual about that.

So I went ahead and took a package of coke over to his place. I was surprised to find that he too was now basing cocaine, since he had always looked down on people who used drugs of any sort. Did he think that I too was spoiled goods?

I sat on the edge of his bed and took the hit he was offering me. Almost before I could exhale, he was on top of me, pinning down my arms and forcing himself on me. I told him no and struggled to get out from under him, but he outweighed me considerably, and his muscle mass was much greater than mine. That was not the only reason I did not fight him off. It was because I would have to turn the ferocity of the energy with which he was now forcing himself on me against him, and it would have been a violent struggle, likely to severely injure us both. Sometimes it comes down to live or die.

So I took it, counting on the coward coming fast. And of course he did, getting off me just as quick. I got up and wandered around his apartment so dazed and so demoralized, too stoned and too ashamed to go home.

He came after me and demanded that I call a whore for him before he would allow me to leave. All of his ruthless darkness continued to rear its ugly head. I didn't know any whores I could call and wouldn't have if I did. He insisted, stupidly, that as I worked in the film industry, I must know someone who knew prostitutes. No idea how he reasoned out that one.

Unfortunately, I did call an actor friend of mine and asked him if he knew any hookers. He said he did not and then he asked me if I was okay. I faltered over my tears to assure him, "Yes, I'm okay."

I was never so humiliated in all my life. I still run into this actor from time to time these days. He has kindly never mentioned the incident to me, and I am always hoping that we are old enough now for at least one of us not to remember. I never told anyone what happened that day, not Roni, not anyone.

I only saw Gingi once again across a crowded room in a dark nightclub, and I wondered if he felt dirty. I wish I could say that was the end of it, that I never put myself at risk again, but it was not. There were still the motels on Ventura Boulevard, getting high with strangers, risking our lives with reckless abandon, the delirium, more and more self-degradation to come, and the total disregard of the holy self I knew to be the truth.

The nights of just doing a few lines were long passed and when I got home, I would lay on my bed in the fetal position, begging God to let me see tomorrow. I hung onto my breath as if it was the anchor of my ship. By some wonderful grace, I woke again after sleeping. Then I would sit and practice the gift, so powerful that it cut through everything. When I stood up, I had my human dignity back, my happiness, and my resolve to continue creating a meaningful life. For a week or two I lived what appeared to be normal. Then the phone would ring, and the roller coaster started up again.

I spent a lot of time smoking with Jack. He was an intellectual and I enjoyed his company. Except that he had this incredibly annoying habit of taking a hit and then wanting to blow it into my mouth. He figured we got double duty out of it that way and insisted that I do the same for him. I actually found it disgusting and it killed the rush for me.

Jack wasn't much for sex while getting high. I am not saying he was never into the sexual aspect, just less, to my great relief. There was that one night I came over to his place, and he said I've got a surprise for you, but you have to be blindfolded. Curiosity got the best of me, and I accepted the blindfold. Then he gently took each of my arms and tied my wrists to the bedposts. I was still intrigued and getting a little excited, as he placed the pipe in my mouth and told me to take a hit.

The next thing I knew he pulled off my pants and went down on me. It was wonderful. We did have a good time that night. When I wasn't sitting on the edge of his bed, I was bouncing around the apartment straightening things up and cleaning. Often, especially with Jack, the anxiety would build, and I would run out of the room.

As Roni became a more and more prominent kingpin, various interesting people wandered through his world like Ike Turner. I met Ike through Roni at a motel on Sunset Strip one night. Marin was fascinated by his musical genius.

He was a deeply thoughtful man and remarkably intelligent, though I don't know why I put it like that, perhaps because his personal reputation beyond the music was that of brutal man. We were all well aware of his turbulent history with Tina. They had broken up some time before but as they shared several children together, they were ever in and out of one another's lives.

Ike would play the keyboard for hours composing new music, improvising as he got high. There always seemed to be an empty sad space in him that I figured was the absence of Tina. She was his one and only love after the music. It's a pity how the broken places in us can break so much around us.

Once he called me to come over to his place in Baldwin Hills. It was a good-sized house, where some of his children lived with him. We never had sex but I did sit and smoke with him for quite a while that night. He enjoyed my presence and liked talking to me.

I guess I dozed off at some point only to be awakened by him violently shaking me. As soon as I became fully conscious, he punched me in the face for absolutely no reason and shoved me into a bathroom, locking the door and saying, "Tina is on her way over. Stay in here and be quiet!"

I don't know how long I was sitting in that bathroom, but I don't think it was longer than an hour.

When he opened the door, he handed me a chunk of cocaine and walked me out saying, "There's a cab out here waiting for you."

I saw that Ike, in his heart of hearts, was someone who wanted to be kind but did not know how. I left and went straight to Roni's.

A couple of months later, at dawn there was a knock at my door. It was Ike. "I need a place to rest." I didn't ask him any questions. Just took him upstairs and let him crash on my bed. I practiced the gift, enjoying the peace within, on pillows across the room and let him sleep it off. Anyone who really knows me, even a little, knows that I am always ready to forgive. He thanked me as he walked out the door, and I never saw him again.

Then there was Micah. He didn't do drugs of any sort but he played an incredibly beautiful guitar. I met him one night when he was playing for Pini. He was fairly handsome with deep-set dark eyes and one of the largest noses I've ever seen. I found him irresistibly sexy, partially because I had been without sex for a long time.

We became lovers quickly though briefly. I was never in love with him. I loved only Zohar, but I had been away from him for a long time now and I wanted the comfort that sex could bring. The relationship was very short-lived but it did get back to Zohar.

I was hanging out with Magdalena around her backyard pool when the phone rang. It was Zohar calling from Israel. How he found me there I do not know. Magdalena handed me the phone and the first words out of his mouth were, "Why are you liar?"

"I am not!" I protested.

There was a long silence. I didn't know what he was referring to, but as the affair with Micah had recently ended, I feared he might have heard about that. Or perhaps he heard about my excessive drug use in America. That would've been confusing enough, as he did not know me to be into drugs, but only as one who practiced the gift. He knew the best of me, so how could anything else be? Zohar broke the silence with a simple question, no recrimination, just a question.

"You want come here?"

"Oh yes!" I said, quietly bursting into tears.

"So come home."

Magdalena was still the manager of the essential oils company, and the company was looking to get involved in lingerie. I found them the perfect designer for the project, and in return I received arms full of gorgeous lingerie. I picked 20 gowns with matching robes for myself and was supposed to sell the bulk of the rest. I crammed the garments into my luggage and headed for Israel.

I arrived at Yona's house in the afternoon before Yom Kippur, hopping out of a cab in front of her house dressed in white from head to toe, as is the mitzvah (blessing). Hofni would soon arrange a place for me to stay in Ramat Gan. Zohar was between places and living at Yona's now. The wonderful large room that was once Zohar's, and where we had celebrated many feasts, had been deconstructed by the city, likely due to it having been built without a permit.

I was standing in Mimi's bedroom unloading the presents I brought for Zohar's sisters, who were anxiously filing into the room as one beautiful garment after another flew over my shoulders to them.

Then suddenly a small, terribly thin man entered the room, and for second I didn't recognize him. It was Zohar, so transformed by the ravages of drugs. He smiled, pleased to see me, and walking over, he fell into my arms. I held him tightly, tears falling from my eyes. I could not believe the weakened condition I'd found him in, but I was quick to dry my tears before he noticed.

Zohar led me into Yona's bedroom where we sat side by side on her bed talking, "Your father died..."

Tears welled up and dripped from my eyes. "Yes."

"I know you loved him very much."

I nodded.

"So did you bring me some Beethoven? I mean Mozart. I lost the Beethoven."

I smiled. "I did bring you some Mozart." I fished it out of my bag and handed it to him. "It's the 'Requiem'."

Zohar mused over the cassette for a moment. "I love Mozart. I saw Amadeus."

"Yes, the music is beautiful, but no music is as beautiful as the music within us."

"I told you, I buy that, but I don't want it."

The next day Yona and I had just returned from the Beit Knesset and were sitting together in the front room when Zohar staggered through the door. Immediately we were on our feet. I noticed a bloodstain on Zohar's pants. Dropping down on one knee, I grasped his pant leg to examine it.

"What is this?"

He pushed my hand away saying gruffly, "Leave it."

Then Zohar began to pass out, caught in our arms. Yona and I carefully walked him to an inside bed. I examined the wound on his leg. It looked as if he had been mauled by a lion. In fact, he had done it to himself. He had ripped through his flesh scratching a deep itch, brought on by the heroin.

The festival of shelters, Sukkot, was fast approaching. Avshalom constructed the frame of the sukkah with a wood frame over the front patio of Yona's house. The structure was then covered with a green tarp on three sides. Colorful paper decorations were scattered on the ground outside. Abigail and I were collecting them, running in and out as we decorated the sukkah for the celebration that evening.

Just outside I saw Zohar strolling towards home and rushed up to greet him. Shyly he said, "I want smoke a little more. You have money?"

"No."

I continued to walk with him for a moment until he said, "So stay here."

Zohar turned and headed in the opposite direction, Avshalom going with him. I headed back to the sukkah until Avshalom came running back after me.

"Come. Zohar wants you."

I followed him to the corner where Zohar began to follow several steps behind us as we continued down the road.

"Zohar needs your jewelry, but he doesn't want to ask you. You'll get it back tonight."

I stood before one of the dealers' houses and tearfully offered up my jewelry to Avshalom with great reluctance, and silently walked away, Zohar still standing in the background.

Later that night I was sitting on the ground in Yona's backyard, cross-legged and crying under the stars. Just then Avshalom appeared. He grasped my hand and placed the jewelry back in my palm. There are few who would promise to return money or valuables, go get high, and hours later care enough to keep their promise.

Zohar was one of the kindest human beings I've ever known. I have been told so many stories about his great heart. Like the time he came out of work, pockets full of cash, and saw a very poor man standing nearby. Zohar took all the cash he had and gave it to the man.

Then there was the time when he was in court waiting to talk to the judge about some minor infraction, and the man ahead of him was given a fine he had to pay on the spot or face jail time. The man pleaded with the judge for time to pay, explaining that he couldn't cover it at that moment, but the judge was unrelenting. So Zohar addressed the judge saying, "I'll pay it for him!" And the man was set free.

Another time at a concert, a man in a wheelchair attempted to come closer to the stage and was being harassed and held back by security. Zohar called down from the stage, "Hey, let him come, that's my brother."

"If I am your brother come down here to me!"

Zohar leapt off the stage and ran to him, embracing him and kissing him.

Zohar was reclining on his mother's bed, very subdued from the heroin he had just finished smoking. I sat at the end of the bed by his feet.

"I think I will have to leave Israel again. It is very hard for me to be here with you as you are now. But if you ask me to stay, if only with your eyes, I will!"

Zohar looked in my eyes, his eyes begging me as tears began to fall from them, but he said nothing.

"Oh, perhaps one day I would find someone, but it would be as if one reaches for the sun and catches but a ray of it!"

Now tears welled up in both of our eyes as we looked deeply into one another lingering in the sadness from which neither of us would ever recover.

I was standing out in front of Yona's house one day waiting for Zohar to return when a young man named Mosihe, who dealt drugs in the neighborhood, walked up to me with one of his friends. The Shikun was sadly overrun with drug addicts and I suppose, as I was with Zohar, they assumed I was one of them.

"At rotsa mah shehu?" ("You want something?")

"Clum." ("Nothing.") I replied

"Kol ha' ha' kavod!" ("All respect!")

"Ze lo kavod. Ze inyan shel hessed." ("It is not about respect. It is a matter of grace.")

"Im zeh lo hiya hah-hessed sheli ("If I had not my grace"), I would be like Zohar."

Mosihe's eyes flashed with admiration. Then the two boys wandered away, and shortly thereafter Zohar sauntered up to Yona's, and sat down silently beside me on the wall of the patio.

"When I showed my father your picture he said, 'He looks like a terrorist'."

Zohar laughed.

"When he heard your voice, he said just one word, 'Great!'"

Zohar's face beamed with pride.

We heard a siren in the background, and for a moment Zohar leapt up, catching his heart, then realizing it was not for him, he went into the house, and I followed behind him.

He found his mother in her bedroom and asked, "You have a goulda?"

Yona sighed but said nothing as she searched through her bedclothes and handed him 10 shekels. The scene frustrated and angered me. Before leaving the room, I turned to Yona and said, "It's not only him. It's us who give him the money for it!"

Then I followed Zohar out of the house, reaching the front step just as he was about to hop in a car with some friends. Zohar stopped before getting in and looked at me over the top of the car. "Stay here!

Our eyes locked in a long last glance, then Zohar jumped into the car, and I watched as he was driven away. I started alone down the quiet desolate street where I would wait for the last bus to come.

When it arrived, I boarded and took a seat in the back of the empty bus. I rested my weary head against the window staring at my own reflection in the glass, tears streaming down my cheeks, I started singing to myself, "Softly as I Leave You".

***

Soon after my return to America, I went to see Roni.

Most of my madness was spent in his house. Marin had left for a few days to get away from him and the drugs. She needed time to regroup, to find herself, to go home in the practice of the gift. As Roni and I sat alone together he talked about Marin. He said the other night she had stripped herself naked and then repeatedly threw her body against the wall. I do remember Marin telling me that once he made her stand outside naked until he would allow her to come back into the house and get another hit. Now he was worried about her.

Marin and Roni went often to the clubs where he could show off his gorgeous woman. She was an extraordinary artist on canvas. She also sang as well as dancing ballet and jazz. Marin was as intelligent as she was stunningly bright. Her smile and happy, gentle mannerisms won the hearts of many. One day she caught the eye of another drug kingpin, Meyer, the boss himself. Roni got wind of it and demanded that Marin stay away from him. But instead she married Meyer, and sometime after I heard she threw herself off a building in Las Vegas.

***

When Roni tired of the subject of Marin, he called a young German girl to join us. And again, the smoking began. This girl, however, was into shooting it. She had brought a couple of syringes with her, and she and Roni were now pumping it up their veins. I too took some shots that night.

I was wandering in the living room for a moment when a loud scream came from the bedroom. I dashed back quickly to find Roni straddled over her lifeless body slapping her ears, weeping, and begging her to wake.

"What happened?" I screamed as I threw him off of her.

"I don't know! She had a seizure, I think."

Now I was at full attention, and every second that followed would forever remain in my memory. She lay motionless on the bed. I have never forgotten the sensation of emptiness that a dead body presents. She was not breathing; there was no heartbeat, no pulse, no energy radiated off her body.

I cried out my favorite prayer for emergencies, "Oh, dear God, please help me!"

I tilted her head back and forced her mouth open, pinning down her tongue with my thumb. I blew five long breaths into her, then I pounded once on her chest with my fist, and then using both hands, palms open, one atop the other, I started the compressions on the sternum to restart the heart, 15 of those, then back to five deep breaths, 15 more compressions, five deep breaths, and then she gasped, drawing breath by herself. Alive again!

She was somewhat dazed, almost frightened coming back. She would always be a little slower, or at least it seemed so to me. She had been out for several minutes after all. I was swept away by the miracle I had experienced at my own hands. It was the first time I had ever performed CPR. My only instruction on how to perform it was years before in a half-hour PBS special.

I was stunned, not only that I could do it but that it worked. It made an indelible impression on me, the fine line between alive and dead. I left, only after I was certain that she was stable. I believe the best to come out of this was that young girl returned to her home to Germany, and I pray she's still there living happily.

Meanwhile, Zohar's life was falling apart. He was all but crawling up to the stage. The unhappiness he brought upon himself was killing him, and he knew it. My father used to say that despair was the only unforgivable sin. Because it meant that one has turned their back on God. And, as we are creatures with free will, from that position we cannot be helped. Buddhists say that it is impossible to take a step backwards in one's knowledge of God. I know that if all the world loves you but you do not love yourself, the world's love cannot save you.

Zohar was apparently arrested on suspicion of stealing a doctor's purse, but was released after it was determined he had nothing to do with the theft. As Zohar was walking out of the jail, he noticed a gun that had been left by an officer on a desk. He picked it up, shoved it in his pants, and continued out the door. In a matter of minutes, the cops realized what had happened and went after him.

He was walking down the street when they caught him a few blocks away. He surrendered the gun without incident. They handcuffed him and took him back to jail. He would be sentenced to several months in prison. I'm not sure how many, maybe six. I could not understand why he had taken the gun, because I knew that he was entirely against weapons. And I was sure that he did not intend to exchange it for drugs. He would not do that. He would not put a gun in someone's hand.

I was heartbroken for him, and I wanted to go to him, but I had no money, as usual. So I continued to look for work in the film industry. I almost ruined all possibility of future work when I showed up late and stoned to a craft services assignment for which my dear friend Jewels had hired me. Up until that day I had never disappointed anyone in any job situation. I always took pride in performing my work, whatever it was, as perfectly as humanly possible.

But on this morning the coffee wasn't there until they had already started shooting. I put my dear friend in the position of having to fire me on the spot. It was a humiliating moment yes, but I was more saddened by the fact that I had disappointed my friend and that she now knew there was something seriously wrong going on in my life. But she gave me another chance.

I was hired for a French car commercial being shot on a racetrack in Riverside. It was a good weeks' worth of work. My job was to get an audience to fill the stadium stands for the mock race. I talked it up at the local universities. I put posters all over town. We got some people, though it wasn't what they were hoping for. Still I played it straight and did a good job.

A month later a check arrived for $1,100, exactly the cost of a flight to Israel round-trip. It was enough to fly there but not enough to live once I got there. So with that as my excuse I decided to take $100 and go buy some coke. And I didn't stop until I had gone through every penny of the $1,100. And then by accident a duplicate check arrived. I knew it was a mistake and that not reporting it would screw the books up for Jewels, but I kept it anyway and said nothing. I spent every penny of that on drugs as well, all the while knowing that Zohar was sitting in jail.

There are not enough pages here to chronicle the days and nights of decadence that I somehow lived through, the neighborhoods I should never have been in, copping drugs. The strangers I hung out with in motels and the unbearable shame that came with lusting after the drug.

Oh, we all thought we were gods when we were high, but we were rabid animals coming down. As I look into so many dark memories, I want to tell them all. No one should think I have not been there or I haven't done that, because I have. In keeping with my fantastic memory, I still remember all of them, their faces and the way they were. I have not forgotten any of them.

I remember one young man whom I was convinced was the reincarnation of St. Thomas. I kept commenting on how much he resembled Thomas, as if I'd known him. What seems important here is that I could see into the core of people's souls and how needlessly we were punishing ourselves. Perhaps I was beginning to develop the compassionate mirror that would ultimately save me.

Years later in Israel I ran into a wonderful woman named Rose. Previously, I had sat with her many long hours, along with Jack and her boyfriend Jeff, now dead, in shabby motels along Ventura Boulevard, smoking the life out of ourselves. Now here she was, sitting with her father in a café looking healthy and beautiful. We recognized each other at once. There we were, both of us standing on our feet, clean and strong. We embraced, so grateful to see each other alive, and she whispered in my ear, "I still have nightmares about that time."

I told her, "Don't let yourself be hurt by it. The dark dreams will fade. You're here. You're alive. We made it!"

I was apartment sitting for the beloved Dizengoff twins, Tami and Rina, while they visited their mother in Israel. I was totally out of control. Rail thin, barely eating, borrowing $20 here and there. I keep remembering this brief scene where I'm in the elevator of the apartment building thinking how pleased I was that I was so thin, when the doors opened and another Israeli friend of mine, an acupuncturist, who was also practicing the gift, stepped into the elevator. I imagine what strikes me so much about that moment was how suddenly terribly ashamed I felt. As if he could see through me. As if he could know the darkness I was now living. Yet there was no judgment in his eyes as we exited the elevator.

He simply said, "Take care of yourself."

I had just returned to their place after another long night of getting stoned when I got the news. Just as I sat down on the living room sofa, the phone rang. It seems that Zohar had been let out on a weekend furlough as a reward for good behavior while in prison. He had stopped the drugs, gained weight, and was giving small concerts for the other inmates.

Why was I not there to greet him, to comfort him, to offer my breast for him to lay his head upon to rest? Alone, first night out, he hooked up with a woman who, hours later, accused him of rape. They found him at his mother's, arrested him, and took him back to the local jail to be taken back to prison. He was likely stoned when they found him and aching for more drugs, crushed beneath the weight of knowing that he would now be going back to prison for a long, long time. How horrible must his pain have been?

***

There was no note left by Zohar… no explanation from anyone, that fit… only the body of work he left behind, in all the notes he sang… for all the children of Israel, whom he loved… and all the world.

***

I don't remember who it was that called and gave me the news. I went immediately into shock. In a daze I sat and wove my hair into one long braid. I secured it at the top and the bottom with rubber bands. Then I took some garden shears that I found in their kitchen, went into the bathroom, and cut my hair off at the nape of my neck. I thought I would send it to Israel and ask Yona to put it in his grave. I did not have the sense to realize it would certainly not get there on time.

I headed back to Roni's saturated in guilt and overwhelmed with despair. Desperate to blame anyone, I conjured up a story on my way there that it was Roni's fault, that he had told Zohar about my other life and it was the reason he had lost all faith. I thank God I did not have a gun because I was so filled with hate and rage, I could surely have killed Roni. Instead I sat again with Marin and him, smoking into the night. Then there was a moment when I wondered, "How much of this do I need to take to die?"

Just then I heard Zohar's voice within me saying, "Don't do it! If you do, it will be a double wrong."

I knew at once that it was him, for no one else would have said it in that way, and it was his voice I heard. Now I knew for sure, that he could see me, and that he was still with me...

But what had I done? And not done?

Chapter Sixteen – Simon

When the world woke to the horrible news, for the next 24 hours every radio station in Israel played only Zohar Argov. I hope he heard it. I know it would have pleased him. He would be proud of that. Zohar was a tortured soul. Out of his depth in some ways and ahead of his time in many others. He started a musical genre, which hundreds of others have tried to emulate. To this day, no one has succeeded. He was larger than life and life could not contain him.

I was not proud of myself. I was wracked with shame, guilt, and the terrifying sense that I could have done something to help him and yet I did nothing, worse than nothing. My beloved one was dead and gone. I would never be able to wrap my arms around his dear sweet, too thin body again. I was beyond inconsolable. My life was now a wasteland. I was empty of all desire. How would I go on living? I and I alone had to live with this guilt. I really don't know if I have ever forgiven myself, and though I do know Zohar wanted me to live a happy life… the shadow of his death stills falls upon me.

My friends tried to tell me, "It's better for you now; he would've taken you down with him." They didn't know him. He would have never let that happen. I took it as a callous comment. How could they say life would be better without the one I loved? Yet where was my love when he needed me the most? How could I ever forgive myself?

What if I had been there when they let him out on furlough? There would've been no one to cry rape. Or would there have been? Would he have stayed with me that night or gone out? Would he have been drawn away from home to the drugs again? Had I not tried to stop him with love for so many years now? Still my mind could not make sense of anything and drove me deeper into the agony of self-recrimination and unbearable guilt.

It was the Dizengoff twins who suggested that Menachem Golan might be interested in a screenplay about Zohar's life. They secured a meeting with him for me, and sure enough he was interested but was not willing to pay to have it written. Nonetheless I decided to go back to Israel and research the screenplay, giving it the working title of *Super Nova*.

I stood in Yona's doorway with my bags at my feet. She had had no idea I was coming but gave me a place to stay in her house that night. Yona was in the deepest stage of grief; her eyes were never without tears. Still for the sake of Zohar she was kind to me. She could see that I too was destroyed.

In the morning, someone from the family directed me to the graveyard, but no one came with me. I was only told that the stone was black. Sometime later it would be covered in white and gray marble, with a guitar carved into the headstone. I never imagined there would be so many graves. How will I ever find him? I wondered.

I closed my eyes for a moment to find him from inside. Then I walked through the rows and down the aisles, directly to the place where he was laid to rest. I fell on my knees and wept. I laid my body upon the cold stone, lamenting. As I got up I used my clothes to clean off the stone carefully. And then I took a small rock and placed it on top of the grave, walking slowly away. I did the same each day until one day I heard his voice say, "Go from here and don't come back! I want you to live!!"

Yona allowed me to stay in her home for a week until Haim kindly offered me the enormous home he had built for his parents with just his one arm. It was right behind the small house they had built together and lived in all their lives.

His father preferred to stay in the small house rather than move into a house built by his junkie son.

Haim had bought himself an old Cadillac that he was very proud of. One Shabbat night he took the car out for a drive. Returning just before dawn, he parked it in his father's driveway and went up to his room to crash. At daybreak he was awakened by the sound of smashing glass. He ran down to see what it was, and sure enough it was his father with a crowbar smashing all the windows of his car. Apparently, he was displeased to find that his son was driving on Shabbat.

The house Haim built was beautiful; the design was artful and extraordinary. It was a four-bedroom on three levels. Downstairs was the great room that included a modern kitchen with black granite counters and off from it, a small bedroom. A granite slab staircase led up to the second level and the wonderful master bedroom I stayed in. Also on this level was a large outdoor patio, a washing machine and a rope to hang laundry. On the very top level was an octagonal room Haim had intended to make into a recording studio, but now it was an open house for many nesting birds. I set about cleaning the kitchen and then started cooking.

Haim's mother Hamama saw me baking chocolate cakes and asked, "How many children do you have?" She had never known anyone to bake so many sweets. But she enjoyed my jachnun, a Yemenite bread that comes out like flaky, caramelized rolls of dough when baked overnight in a warm oven for breakfast on Shabbat. Each Saturday she invited her girlfriends over to have some. Everyone agreed it was excellent, shocked that an American was able to make it, the many layers "gam sefer", like a book. The fact that these old ladies would leave their jachnun at home and come to eat mine was an incredible compliment. Hamama kindly taught me to make her Yemenite soup in return.

Every Friday I spent cleaning the house fastidiously and preparing the evening meal for Shabbat. The jachnun itself took more than an hour to prepare, involving many turns of the dough before it was ready to be placed in the oven-house to get. The dinner itself would include two loaves of challah bread, two entrees, and then dessert. I shopped the day before, buying everything that was needed including the wine for Kiddush.

One time, Haim invited his two children and a cousin to join us. Everyone enjoyed the rare feast. When dinner was over and everything was put away, I took a glass goblet of wine upstairs, placed it on the nightstand, and then went quickly to sleep. Haim had stayed to watch TV downstairs. Something woke me, and my astral form snuck quietly down the stairs to see what it was. There was Zohar sitting next to Haim watching him watch TV. As if in a dream state, I saw nothing abnormal here. I went back upstairs quietly so as to remain unnoticed and fell back to sleep.

In the morning I was shocked to find the crystal goblet had exploded, though the stem still stood exactly where I had placed it. Shattered glass in tiny chunks was scattered everywhere on the wine-drenched floor. I was completely nonplussed by the sight of it. I had never seen anything like it, and it seemed physically impossible. I didn't muse over it long before I realized that Zohar must had been in my room, as I remembered seeing him downstairs the night before. Was it a message from him of anger or his own despair? I know he wanted me to know he had been there. I ran downstairs and out to the small front house to get Haim.

"Come, I want to show you something."

"I don't want to see it!" he said immediately.

"Haim, you have to see this!"

"No! I know he has been here but after a year he will not be able to come here anymore!"

In Judaism it is believed by some that the soul is at liberty to walk the earth for one year after death. This is the reason why the memorial stone is often not placed on the grave until the year has passed.

I pressed on telling Haim, "I have never seen anything like this!" Haim followed me into the big house and up the stairs. I brought a broom with me. He was shaken by the sight, and I think a little afraid. He turned around and left, grumbling inaudibly on his way out the door.

My lovely master bedroom, complete with private bath, had a large four-poster bed, a nightstand, an armoire, and a desk situated under the window overlooking the orange grove. It was sitting there that I began to construct the outline of the screenplay. I arranged appointments for interviews with Zohar's family and friends, some of whom were his colleagues, his managers, and nightclub owners. Rare was the person who knew him that did not count himself among his friends. I even heard about the young man from Bat Yam, who committed suicide when he heard that Zohar had died. I was sad for him, though not surprised.

It was six months later, on a bus headed to the main station in Tel Aviv, when I first realized I was still alive. I remember the exact moment. I saw the sunlit leaves glistening on a tree and I knew I would soon rejoin the world of the living.

Later, standing outside on the patio deck having just finished hanging clothes on the line, I stood quietly looking out over the tiny village that was Zohar's home. I still felt as if my life was a wasteland. Aside from completing the screenplay, there was nothing more I wanted. No further direction I could see or longed to follow.

Then suddenly I heard a knock, as clear as if a hand was tapping on wood, and then again. I looked around to see where it was coming from. Looking down I realized the knock was coming from within me, inside my solar plexus. Then a voice spoke softly yet clearly from within, "I want to come back into life."

Though I have never been someone who heard voices, I listened carefully as it was repeated again.

"I want to come back into life!"

I recognized the voice of this soul wanting to come through me. I never really doubted who it was.

"Okay," I thought. *"But I have no father for you!"*

Within a day the couple that lived across the street from Zohar's mother called me at Haim's. They asked if I'd be interested in going out dancing with them some night that week. Since Zohar was not yet dead a year by Jewish law there was some question about whether I should be dancing at all, but I accepted the invitation anyway.

When I arrived at their home that night, Mini, Shlomi's wife, announced that she wasn't feeling well enough to go and did I mind that her husband planned on bringing someone with him? Evidently, it was supposed to be a foursome that had now turned into a threesome, the two boys and me. I shrugged my shoulders. It was okay. I was going to dance no matter what.

Then she added, "Do you like monkeys?"

"Excuse me?"

"Simon, he is very hairy," she announced with considerable disgust, grinning as she moved her hands up and down her body to indicate that he was hairy all over.

I shrugged my shoulders again and said, "What do I care? I dance alone!"

"You dance alone?" she asked, somewhat alarmed.

Shlomi motioned towards the door and I left without answering. How was I so naïve that I still hadn't realized it was a set up?

Simon's home was outside the Yemenite village close to the center of Rishon Le Zion. It was a small Swiss cottage sitting in an ample yard surrounded by apartment buildings. I remember the look on his face when he opened the door. It was a flash of doubt and concern just before he remembered his manners, ushering us in and introducing himself to me as Simon. He wasn't quite ready yet and asked us to wait a moment. Aggravated, perhaps by feeling rushed, he disappeared into the back room and returned moments later looking as dapper and ready as he possibly could. He vaguely resembled Omar Sharif.

Simon was a mix of Iraqi and Adeni blood, born in Mumbai. He played it very cool. We went to a large discotheque just outside a town where I had never been before. I had never been to a discotheque in Israel nor did I even know they existed. Zohar was a ballad singer. He sang in nightclubs, weddings, and at bar mitzvahs. He was and is the folk soul of Israel.

We got a good table, ordered some drinks, and I asked for cigareem. These are a bit of spiced meat or vegetables rolled up in filo dough to resemble cigars. After being fried to a golden brown, they are usually dipped in tahini as they are eaten and are a good accompaniment to a stiff drink.

Simon got a weird look on his face and made some comment like, "You like to eat?" I got the impression that it was improper for me to order something for the table unless I planned to pay, which I did, not realizing I was their guest. Still, as their guest I would be inclined to order what I wanted.

Then came the big surprise, he asked me to dance, and oh God, could he dance! We started dancing to a song called "Jessica". Samba, mambo, tango, or just plain rock and roll, Simon was a wonderfully exciting, amazing dancer! We had great fun together that night. It was intoxicating. When we went outside for a smoke, he kissed me and I kissed him back. He asked if he could call me, and I said yes.

Simon called the next day and invited me to a barbecue on the beach that night, explaining that it was just a gathering of friends, primarily cops and cabdrivers. He picked me up in front of Haim's house. When we arrived, there were about 20 people casually dressed sitting around folding chairs and tables.

The fires were burning bright, and meat was on the grill. Everyone had brought something and there was an abundance of salads, tahini, pita, wine and beer. I was planning to interview some of the cops regarding Zohar's death in the Rishon police station.

When I shared that idea with Simon as we sat down with our first drink of the night, he protested, "Don't be stupid!"

I said nothing and had every intention of doing as I pleased, but I missed the red flag. There is little I like less than a man telling me what I may or may not do and using the word "stupid" in reference to me was as ridiculous as it was unspeakably rude. That he thought he could say that, should have been a warning that this was not the man for me, that he would never know me nor be able to control me.

However, he was very well built and I suppose a little sexy. His hands were as gruff as they could be though able to move delicately. I could see that he was proud to be with me.

There were whispers of Zohar's name throughout the night. I responded by confronting one of the cops. I asked him how it was that Zohar could have killed himself in his jail cell. Do they not watch over the prisoners who are obviously at risk? When he cried out a second time for a doctor did it occur to anyone that perhaps a psychiatrist was needed? And is it true that your captain lost his job two weeks later?

At that point Simon jumped in, leading me away and telling me, "Leave it alone."

Simon kissed me several times before he asked if I would come with him. I was hot and hungry and so I did. Just as we approached his home he asked, "Are you the one

I've been waiting for? I pray to God you are the one I have been waiting for."

His house was absolutely charming. It had an open front porch, and you entered into the kitchen, which had plenty of counter space and a snack bar area with two barstools. The living room was roughly furnished with wood-frame couches and chairs with cushions. Sliding black-framed glass doors separated the bedroom area, which included a large master bedroom and another L-shaped room beyond that. We were soon making love on his king-size bed.

As I grasped his buttocks to draw him closer to me, I noticed a very thick scar and I could not help but ask in the middle of everything, "Were you wounded?"

He whispered, "It's like a wound."

It turned out it to be an untreated case of acne conglobate, an uncommonly severe form of acne, characterized by burrowing and interconnected abscesses and cysts containing a foul-smelling seropurulent material that returns after drainage and causes heavy scarring. Draining it for him would one day fall upon me.

Meanwhile, Mimi had been right about the hair. He was sweating heavily in the midst of our passion, and for me it was like swimming on a carpet. Still in some ways it was the best sex we would ever have. He would never kiss me again like that, and I would never know why.

***

The next afternoon Simon called to ask if I would join him and his son at the beach the following day. Just the fact that he would pick me up in front of Haim's house in the middle of the day created quite a scandal in the little village. But I was totally oblivious to that. I had troubles of my own.

The money I had so freely thrown around was now gone. It came to the point where I was hungry and had no money to buy food. I was lucky I had a roof over my head.

I tried to get anyone to help me from outside Israel. I think my mother sent me a little money. It got so bad that I called my brother John and pleaded with him to send me $20 and to ask each of my brothers and my sister to do the same. But no help came.

I spent my last few shekels to get to Jerusalem. There I sold a ring that Patty had given me to a jeweler. It was a beautiful modern setting of several pretty diamonds in white and yellow gold. Selling it gave me enough money to eat for another few days. By now I was mostly on a diet of bread and cheese, which is not a great suffering, but I was worried about nutrition.

When Simon picked me up that Saturday morning, he noticed the ring was gone and he suspected what had become of it, but said nothing at that moment. In the car with him was a beautiful bright brown-eyed boy with lovely black hair and gorgeous golden-brown skin. I don't think I'd ever seen a more handsome little boy. He was a little shy at first. I asked him in Hebrew what his name was, and he told me after his father encouraged him.

"David."

"David? I like that name!"

He smiled. Simon insisted we stop by Shlomi and Mini's house to have some jachnun. Mini made hers with honey, more like a sweet roll, so not possible to dunk it into a spicy tomato sauce, though she did offer tahini with it. I didn't like it as well as mine but I didn't say anything. David was enjoying it, so all was well. I really could not get over what a beautiful boy he was. I would later learn that he was the second youngest of Simon's six children from his three wives. I noticed that Simon treated David gently for the most part and that he had extraordinary patience with him.

On our way to the beach I learned that after the Israelis had gained control of Israel, scouts were sent out around the world looking for young Jewish boys near bar mitzvah age. They went as far as Mumbai where Simon's family lived. His father was a textile merchant. When he would visit his father's factory, the workers bowed their heads to Simon with folded hands as they filed by him. It was a sign of respect for the owner's son.

Simon did not really get along with his father and so when the scouts came and asked if he was interested in coming to Israel, Simon said yes. Because his brother David was already there, his parents allowed him to go.

Once in Israel he would be raised on a kibbutz and trained to be a farmer and a soldier. His education would go no further than that, and believe me, he lived to resent it, but he would always love Israel more than his own mother.

On the beach, I played with David. I felt instantly drawn to him and I genuinely liked him. He was cheerful, smart, and very loving. We became extremely close in just a few hours by the sea.

Later that afternoon we sat together on the front porch at his father's home. He looked into my eyes, smiling, and asked me in Hebrew, "Do you love Daddy?"

I smiled at him and said, "I love you!"

"And Daddy?"

"Yes."

I stayed to have dinner with them. We made a wonderful barbecue together. Simon took care of the meat, and I made my fabulous tahini and added fries to the meal. David was having a grand old time. He loved me, and I loved him too. I started looking at Simon as a father. I watched the way he behaved with David.

I asked Simon how it was that he allowed David to tell him "No!" so often? He said, "This is a very difficult world, and I want him to grow up to be someone who will not take no for an answer."

I thought something in his parenting must be working because David was a strong little boy, high-spirited, with a mind of his own. I would use what I was learning here in the near future. I stayed with Simon that night, and David was delighted to find me still there in the morning. I made him a quick breakfast, helped him get ready for school, and kissed him on his way out the door.

Simon asked if he could visit Zohar's grave with me before dropping me back at my house. I was touched and surprised by his suggestion, and so I agreed to it. Perhaps he wanted Zohar to know that he would take care of me, or perhaps it was just to let him know that he was with me now. He followed just a step behind me as I led him to my precious Zohar's grave. I kissed the marble and placed a stone. Simon prayed silently for a moment, then he too placed a stone, and we walked out of the graveyard without a word.

Back in the car he asked about the ring, knowing I had sold it. I told him the truth, and he asked if I would like to come and live with him and David for the duration of my stay in Israel. I told him I would think about it. When I arrived home, all hell broke loose with Haim. Perhaps he thought I had given up mourning Zohar too soon. He was wrong. I have never stopped mourning him. I packed my bags and called Simon to come pick me up.

I quickly settled into this lovely little family like a baby propped on cushions in a cradle. I was brain-dead from the weight of tragedy, and all I really needed now was comfort, kindness, and good food. I got much more than that. Simon fell in love with me, and David loved me as much as I loved him from the start. Simon must've figured out the fastest way to keep me was to get me pregnant. So one day as I was gazing at David with love, he asked, "Do you want me to make one for you?"

I had heard that before, though it was put a little differently because it was Zohar, who seeing me holding an infant said, "You want I make one like that for you?"

I started my jachnun on Thursday, and on Friday I prepared a feast such as they had never seen in that house before. I encouraged Simon to invite some friends. I served Trout Almondine, orange duck, two loaves of challah, several different vegetables, and dessert. Playing hostess/chef is always a pleasure in itself. I delighted in the joy of my guests as they ate the meal I prepared.

Unfortunately for me when one is not educated, usually their friends are not either. They were sweet, kind people, and I thought that they were very dear but the conversation was entirely about the Toto, which is the Israeli version of the Lotto. Hence, the discussion was centered around football teams and who would win that Sunday. Simon highly praised me to all of them, holding the chalice of kiddush wine and reciting the prayer about how a good wife is worth more than rubies. He honored me, or so I thought. I remember him telling me once, "You shall be my queen and I shall be your king!" Sounds romantic at first, but what does it mean? I did not know nor did I ask myself, though I would soon find out.

In some way, it was clear that Simon was doing everything he could to connect with me, to keep me. He even came with me into Tel Aviv one night to hear about the gift. He did not simply dismiss it out of hand. Nor did he denounce it at the first meeting. There were a relatively small number of people practicing the gift in Israel at that time. A young Israeli man I knew from Los Angeles happened to be there at the same time. Yoram was secretly organizing an event for the Teacher to come and speak.

I received a call one day telling me to come to a woman's apartment in Tel Aviv. I waited in the living room until taken back to her bedroom where I was asked to sit next to my friend, Yoram, who whispered in my ear, "Tel Aviv Hilton."

It was to be a two-day event, Saturday and Sunday. I would not understand the need for such secrecy until the event was over and the Monday morning newspapers came out. The police had originally hoped to stop him at the border not realizing that his passport would be under his given name. Perhaps the message he brought was considered inappropriate for the mindset of Israel at that time.

All the while the event was going on, the police were hunting for him in the bar mitzvah and wedding halls, never imagining he would be at the Hilton.

Simon put me into a cab he'd called for me the first morning of the event. The same driver would be waiting to pick me up that evening. It occurred to me on my way into Tel Aviv that the Teacher might open the floor to questions again. At the same time I told myself, "You must not raise your hand. You must not take time away from these people who so rarely have a chance to see him."

We met with him, all 200 of us, in a small ballroom. It was a great relief to me, as it was the first time I'd seen him since Zohar died. He started talking about death. I actually sat on my hands to keep from raising them, but the moment he asked for questions my hand shot up, and he called on me immediately.

I stood up and told him everything that had happened. That if anyone had ever told me that after receiving his gift I would want to die, I would have thought it impossible. But when my beloved died, I walked among the dead, and the only thing that saved me was his gift that had been revealed to me. It was the glue that held me together, the undeniable truth I could not dismiss. And that I knew I would be okay when I saw the light dancing on the leaves. So I thanked him profusely for this wonderful gift and then I shut my mouth.

Unlike the many friends who said, "Better for you he's dead," my Teacher simply said, "I was eight years old when my father died, and to tell you the truth, if it happened today, I don't know what I would do."

I was so touched by his compassion and humility.

There was a break shortly afterwards, and some people approached me, knowing that I had been speaking of Zohar, though I don't know for certain how they knew. Many sweet condolences were given. When I returned to my seat, I found that someone had left a chocolate bar there called Evergreen.

When I returned home, Simon's primary interest was whether or not the cabdriver had tried to start with me. The next morning, he drove me himself and picked me up afterwards.

The Teacher did something I had never seen him do before nor have I ever seen him do since. He said that he had written a poem in the night and he would like to read it to us.

It was an exceptionally long piece of ecstatic prose. The refrain was, "Remember though the lover may perish the love never dies." That phrase lifted me from tragedy and carried me through the sorrows yet to come.

My love for David grew deeper. He and Simon were both fascinated by my healing powers. David wanted to learn, and he was a quick study, possibly because in a child's mind there was nothing to stop him from doing what came most naturally. So he observed me holding my hands just above someone's body in a certain area, and somehow he got it. And he started to do the same for real, not just playing at it.

More and more I looked at Simon as the possible father of my child, and he was willing. Aside from the monkey fur, he had a strong, almost perfect body and a million-dollar butt. I used to enjoy watching him walk, staying a step behind him. I'm sure he thought I was walking behind him out of respect but I was just watching his ass. He could also have chewed rocks with his teeth. So he looked like good stock. He asked me to marry him while driving the car, and I agreed staring out the windshield saying, "Yes." With the provision, "If you can get me pregnant."

"No problem. I have very strong zerah (sperm)!"

So we began trying to get pregnant. The first month it didn't catch. The second month, which was just before I was leaving in late August, also failed. I broke down when

I started my period after the second chance. My heart goes out to those women who try over and over again only to repeatedly find they are not pregnant. I am sure it is heartbreaking, to say the very least.

I had been in Israel almost nine months when I went to the American consulate for help with repatriation. As I was an American citizen virtually stranded with no money and unable to return to the United States, the American Embassy was often willing to help in such cases. I felt I had to get back to the States to settle my affairs and formally make Aliyah. I would have to complete the paperwork from the States that would allow me to return to Israel as a citizen. Israel, as far as I know, is one of the few countries left where you are allowed to hold dual citizenship.

Simon needed much convincing that I would be coming back. He and David took me to the airport. We all kissed and hugged, and holding back the tears, I waved to them as the escalator took me up to Departure.

Once back in the States I got wasted a few more times, mostly with Jack. What made me rush back to it after so long without it? The haunting of addiction. Jack and I made love a few times when we got high, including just days before I would be returning to Simon in Israel. Of all the wrong I might have done him, it was going back to Simon that he would never forgive me for. I had scheduled my return in early December to arrive exactly when I would be ovulating.

I arrived at the Israeli Customs wearing a lady's navy two-piece Don Loper suit from the early '50s and a matching hat with the net over my face, as Simon had requested. Despite the fact that I had my Aliyah papers with me and everything was in order, I was not allowed to pass. Instead,

I was taken to a small room where it was explained to me that there was a suspicion that perhaps I was a spy. I had to hide the secret thrill I felt being placed in that category. It was absurd, but I have long suspected it had something to do with that night I cross-examined the cops at the beach on my first date with Simon. It wasn't until Simon arrived claiming me as his wife that they let me go and my immigration was complete.

Simon and David were so sweet, so happy to see me. Simon and I made love that night, and just before we came together Simon cried out to the child, "Come on! We want you!"

I conceived that night.

As soon as I missed my period, we went to the doctor. The excellent news was that I was pregnant. The unfortunate news was that the HGC levels were too low for the baby to survive. It was a Friday afternoon. He told me to come back on Monday, he would check again, and I shouldn't be surprised if I soon miscarried.

We spent a quiet Shabbat together, David, Simon, and me. Clinging gently to one another, each of us was hoping and praying that the child would be okay so we would be a family.

On Sunday, Simon came into the kitchen just before leaving for work to announce that our friend Raymond, a rabbi, had died in his sleep the night before. Simon continued to explain that Raymond had been in the hospital for several days since I had arrived. He hadn't told me because he was afraid that I would go to the hospital and do another healing on Raymond, as I had so many times before. He warned me, "Don't go there!"

I waited until he left, then I locked up the house and headed over to Raymond's to pay my respects. His rather large home, by comparative standards in the neighborhood, was full of people on the floor, wall to wall "sitting shiva". I approached his wife to express my condolences, then took my place with the others on the floor. In Judaism it is customary to sit shiva for seven days after the death of a family member, and it is also a mitzvah (blessing) to eat.

Soon wonderful Indian food was being passed around much to my unabashed delight. Once I had my fill, I paid my final respects to the family and quietly left. As I headed back home crossing the glen between our homes, I heard a voice telling me, "The child will be well."

I knew immediately that it was Raymond and that perhaps it was his moment to help me and my baby. Shortly after I returned home, Simon came bursting through the front door.

"I can see I'm going to have trouble with you."

"What do you mean?"

"I watched you leave the house. I was parked on the street. You disobeyed me and went to Raymond's anyway."

I was somewhat stunned. First that he was spying on me, and worse, that he thought I would obey him! He defended his position saying, "I did not want you to go because I was afraid when you saw his wrapped body lying on the sidewalk you might be shocked and lose the baby."

"What body? I never saw it."

The next day we returned to the doctor, who took another blood test. The HGC count had soared so high, there was no doubt the pregnancy was well on. I was thrilled though not surprised. There was just one little problem. The contraceptive sponge I used when making love to Jack had torn, and there was a small doubt in my mind as to whose child this really was. Very unlikely to be Jack's, but I was not 100% certain. Of course, I never told Simon about my doubt.

I really tried to adjust myself to the quiet simple life I had agreed to in our little family. But I was homesick for America and my mother. I explained to Simon that I wanted to go home and see my mother before settling in permanently. He was afraid that probably I would not come back, but at the end of long negotiations he agreed to let me go. When Simon took me back to the airport, David and I were both in tears. I promised him I would be back soon. The Joan Baez song "Jesse" was playing in my head as I waved goodbye. It was then and there that I decided to name my child Jessi.

Mother was not exactly thrilled to see me. She guessed before I told her that I was pregnant by a man she had never met. Moreover, I was unmarried. I told her we were planning to be married when I returned but I was getting bigger and bigger without a ring on my finger.

I told Simon it was embarrassing, but that was met with hostility and anger. I found it so humiliating I went and bought a ring for myself. It was cubic zirconium, but it looked nice, and no one really knew the difference. The cross-continental arguments escalated, and when the phone bill arrived it was $700. My mother was furious. I somehow managed to pay it with no help from Simon. He sent me a one-way ticket to return.

I was supposed to come back with money. I had hoped to get an advance on the screenplay but no such luck. I returned penniless to Israel, and Simon was more than disappointed.

By now I was six months pregnant. Despite all the many fights over the phone, Simon had really made valiant efforts to prepare for my return and the arrival of our child. He had built a nursery off David's room. The crib was already there waiting. He also put screens on all the windows to keep the giant bugs from flying in. He had said nothing about these preparations. He wanted to surprise me, and he really did. He had my favorite seven-layer cake waiting for me. David was overjoyed to see me. He clung to me, his beautiful sweet smiling face beaming. They put a candle in the cake asking me to make a wish and blow it out.

Simon said, "You were never loved more."

Later that first night of my arrival, the 1936 black-and-white version of Dostoyevsky's Brothers Karamazov played on TV. I was not yet tired, even though it was nearly midnight when the show began, and it was a film I'd never seen before from the work of my favorite novelist, so I was interested but Simon was entirely bored. My trying to explain the various themes to him somehow made it even less comprehensible. The fact that I was interested in such heady literature seemed to annoy him. Another red flag waved before my eyes, and again I tried not to see it.

The next morning, I helped David get ready for school, as I had done so many times before. When he was all slicked up and ready to go, he took a seat at the kitchen snack bar, where I served him tea and pita bread with Nutella, his favorite breakfast. He had a very concerned look on his face as he tried to ask me something in Hebrew.

"Daddy told me that if things don't go well between you two, you would go but your child would stay here. Is that true?"

I am sure a very serious look flashed across my face. "Come with me."

I took David gently by the hand and led him into our bedroom where Simon was just waking. I told David in Hebrew, "Tell your father what you have just told me."

And to Simon I said, "I want to be sure that I understood him correctly."

David shyly repeated to his father what he had said to me, and a sickening grin appeared on Simon's face. This was the beginning of the end. After all I had already lost to Israel, if anyone thought I would lose my child here, they would have to think again. I could not take that threat lightly. I tried to reason with him. I told him that if you hang a machete blade by a hair above the head of a guest at a fabulous banquet, he would not be able to enjoy his dinner. All the while he remained silent and unrelenting.

That weekend there was another surprise waiting for me. Simon had bought a small restaurant at the local country club. His plan was that we would work it as a family. Knowing that I was an excellent cook he figured there could not be a problem with this.

I had only been there for a few days and was extremely jetlagged. It was the middle of May. The temperature was nearly 100 degrees with 100% humidity. I was miserable and unable to show proper appreciation for our new situation. I spent the entire afternoon sitting in the shade and wiping sweat off my brow.

Needless to say, Simon was quite disappointed in what he perceived as a lack of appreciation for his efforts to please me, and I can understand why. He had sunk what little money he had into acquiring the snack bar, and now it seemed as if I wasn't even interested. The only flight he had taken in his life was when he was 12 years old and had journeyed to Israel. He had no concept of jetlag or pregnancy despite the fact that he had already sired six children, and mine was the seventh. Simon's frustration with me became smoldering anger.

Despite the fact that he had built a nursery for our baby, he hadn't thought to have the kitchen cleaned. The inside of the cupboards were filthy and scattered with the remains of dead cockroaches. I needed some sort of cleaning product but there was none, and there was also no money to buy any except for a bowl of change up on one of the kitchen shelves. I took the change, went across the street, and bought a large bottle of concentrated cleaning fluid.

When Simon returned from the office that night, I explained to him what I had done, and he was livid. It wasn't long before he was screaming, ranting, and raving. It eventually came down to that I had promised to return from America with money, and where was it? He seemed to be under the impression that all Americans are wealthy and easily able to access any needed funds. He could not be convinced that I did not have the ability to bring him more money. I had already given everything I had on my last trip there.

When I realized there was no reasoning with him, I walked out of the room and called a Russian woman I had met on the airplane coming over. He heard me complaining to her about him, and worse than that, I called him an idiot. For him that declaration was an unforgivable sin. Never mind that it was said in anger. I could not take it back, even though I attempted to, and he could not forgive me.

"Okay, so now I do not want to marry you and I want you to leave. If you do not leave, I will take all of your things, throw them outside, and set them on fire!"

Fortunately, I had not yet unpacked, but unfortunately, I had no money, and in the morning when he left for the office, he took the phone with him. I was completely desolate and desperate. I knew nothing about the film *Not Without My Daughter*, but I was going through a similar circumstance in Israel. My own mother did not have the ability to help me, and so I was forced to beg my aunt, one of my father's sisters, to help me. Reluctantly, she agreed to send me just enough for a plane ticket and not a penny more.

In the days that I waited for the bank transfer, I went back to the pregnancy clinic for an ultrasound. In the earlier stages of my pregnancy, they tried to insist that I have an amnio test. When I refused, they looked at me as if I was crazy. In Israel it is very much about survival of the fittest. After all, I was 36, and it was considered a high-risk pregnancy. I told them that I was keeping this child no matter what. As the ultrasound scope rolled over my stomach the nurse cheerfully announced, "Ah, you have a girl!"

"No, it's a boy," I exclaimed automatically.

She repositioned the scope and pointed out, "This is a girl!"

When I left the office, I walked along the sidewalk caressing my stomach and saying, "I am so sorry, Darling, I thought you were a boy! Now what shall I name you?" And then it struck me, "Jessica, of course, Jessi for short!"

Years later I would understand why I thought I had wanted a boy. I wanted my child to have an easy life. I thought, as a girl, if she is beautiful that will be a problem. Not so beautiful, another problem. If she has a beautiful body, that too will be a problem. Not such a beautiful body, again another problem. And if she's intelligent, that will be a real problem; if not intelligent, even worse. But a man can be short, fat, bald, ugly, and stupid, and it's still not necessarily a problem.

My last few days in Simon's house were brutally sad. One evening he called me from work to say, "Make dinner for yourself if you like, but not for David and me. If you do, I will throw it in the trash."

One of his sons, Yaad, a 17-year-old soldier whom I had befriended, turned his back on me as well. He would sit in the front room with his father and his heartless girlfriend, Revetal, laughing and joking, making fun of my pitiful condition. My intense sorrow was a source of great amusement for them all. I finally realized that all I needed was a phone, any phone, and I would be able to plug it into the jack on the kitchen wall and call my mother to let her know I was coming home. So I went to a neighbor who had been kind to me and asked her to please let me take her phone back to Simon's for just a little while. As luck would have it, Simon arrived home for lunch just as I was calling Mother. He grabbed the handset out of my hands, ripped the phone out of the wall, and tore the gold chain off my neck saying, "This will help pay your phone bill." Then he stormed out of the house.

I ran to a neighbor, who had often been a guest at our table on Shabbat, and asked him to let me use his phone. I called the Russian woman and asked if I could come to her house for just a few days until my plane took off. She said I was welcome, but that I would have to arrive quickly as she and her husband were leaving within the hour for a vacation to her family's home in Australia. I had to ask the good neighbor to please give me 20 shekels and call me a cab.

He kindly agreed and would lose his friendship with Simon for helping me to escape. Then I went back to the house and put all of my things at the front door for the driver to take. I took the six fine wine goblets I had bought for Simon's birthday, put five of them in a large bucket to take with me as a gift for the Russian, and kept one goblet aside. I took the glass-framed photograph off the wall of Simon and me in Haifa at New Years and placed it on the kitchen counter. I then laid the goblet down on top of it, placed a kitchen towel over both, took a hammer and smashed them. I removed the towel to reveal the shattered glass, put the hammer away, and walked out the door.

Sadly, it was that very morning when I had sat David down and told him I would soon have to leave and that it did not mean I did not love him. I told him I loved him and that I would always love him, and that if anything ever happened to his father, I would come back for him. I asked him if he understood me. He just nodded his head sadly. We were both weeping. I hugged him and kissed him and sent him off to school. Leaving him was one of the hardest things I have ever done in my life. I loved him as my own son, and even now I carry him in my heart, yet I have not seen him since. My departure broke his heart, and the damage would permanently color his life.

When I arrived at the Russian's apartment, they were just walking out the door. In fear of errant calls, they had taken out the phone and the TV as well. There was barely a scrape of food anywhere either. Whatever few shekels I had left, I spent on a little bread and cheese. It would be two more days before my flight left for the States. I spent most of the time hiding in the barren apartment, praying that Simon would not find me.

I do not even recall how I got to the airport, as I had no cab fare. Possibly the kind neighbors, who had given up their friendship with Simon to help me, came and got me. I only know that once at the airport I managed to scrape up enough change to call Simon. Now it was my turn to threaten him. I told him I was leaving and that I would never let him get within a hundred yards of my child. I was surprised to hear the contrite sorrow in his voice.

He said, "I've heard you have a little girl. I am happy for you. Please tell me where you are. Please meet with me somewhere. I want to talk with you, to see you. Please."

Instinctively I knew had I told him I was at the airport, he would have easily had me detained. In Israel he had as much right to the child as I did, and it was not legal for me to take the child out of the country without both of us agreeing to it. Further as I was now in my seventh month, there might have been some question as to the advisability of boarding a plane.

So I just said, "It's too late."

I hung up the phone and boarded the plane, weeping all the way.

Looking back now, decades later, I can imagine when Simon returned home that day and saw the shattered goblet and glass over our destroyed photo, he must have felt the deep agony of another failed relationship, and I imagine he wept.

Chapter Seventeen – Jessi

Many men in my life asked me to marry them, and then after I declined came back to ask if I would at least have their child, each explaining, "Because your child will be extraordinary." I chose the one who just happened to show up when I needed him.

My mother was slightly less than thrilled to see me so pregnant and so unmarried. Neither one of us could have imagined such a thing happening in our family. I would never know what it might have been like to have a loving husband by my side to protect and care for me. Moreover, Mother detested Simon for so many reasons, I was concerned she might never accept this child.

My mother's place was a doublewide mobile home in a retirement park for people fifty and over. Her unit was especially large. There was a large living room, an adjoining dining room with a built-in hutch, an ample kitchen with a breakfast nook, a small den, two bedrooms each with their own bath, and a master bedroom that included a small vanity area. My little brother Joe had never left home and lived in the second bedroom. He was just turning 30 and had long suffered from clinical depression. He tried to medicate himself with alcohol and the occasional joint. He would go out at night and drink beer until he could barely see, and

Mother would wait up for him until the wee hours of the morning when he finally stumbled through the door. It was a dance they had been doing for many years now since my father died. Mother lived in constant fear of Joe dying because of his drinking. My brother Bill said of Joseph, "He can't drink and he can't drive and gets in the car and tries to do both!"

I slept, when I was able to, on the sofa in the living room until the child came. In the sleepless hours I would gently stroke my stomach to comfort the child, and I swear I could feel her hands caressing the wall inside to comfort me.

We were now at the mercy of my mother and the state of California. As I was penniless, I would have to go on welfare. Having arrived back in the States with very few prenatal medical records and all of those written in Hebrew, it was extremely difficult to find a doctor who would take me as a patient. After twenty doctors refused me, I got back in Mom's car and broke down. But she would not have that. She was strong and encouraged me to be the same.

"You'll find someone. Come on; don't worry. It's going to be all right."

Her kindness and gentleness would pass through the genes to my wonderful daughter, now well on her way to me.

I finally found Dr. T. T. Lee, a doctor not far from Mother's home. He took the case and sent me to a special prenatal clinic, where they kept close watch over the child's progress in bi-weekly visits. There were many ultrasounds, and in each one she was peacefully floating, sucking her thumb, a habit she had only in the womb and once out, would never resume.

I recall one day a prayer crossed my mind, what I most hoped for my child. "Lord, let me bring forth a blessed one!" I had no concept of what that would mean, but the gifts she was born with were beyond anything I could have thought to request.

As I got bigger in the last months, I often wished there was a crane above the sofa to help pull me up. I had always thought pregnancy would be easy for me, but it was not. It brought meaning to the concept of a woman as a cow. It connected me to my animal self in a way that I had never imagined. And then there was the realization that I would never be just myself again. I wasn't sure how I would handle that. Yet I would soon discover that she was the grace of my life.

Back at the prenatal clinic there were concerns about possible complications. I had been suffering from severe headaches. My father had had an aortic aneurysm, supposedly the size of a sausage, though I never knew whether that meant breakfast or kielbasa. It was discovered in the year before his death and had developed over thirty years. He was never told he had it. Aside from his doctor, only mother knew about it, and if it burst, he would bleed to death in a minute and a half. The hereditary possibility was taken into consideration by my doctor and as I was too big now to fit in an MRI, there was no way to determine if the severe headaches I was having were because of a brain aneurysm. So the decision was made to deliver by C-section on her due date.

Mother took me to the hospital early in the morning on the day of delivery. They shaved and catheterized me while

I waited to be taken to surgery. Then they rudely put me on a scale so that I could discover I had gained 40 pounds! I was stripped naked and asked to hunch over while the anesthesiologist attempted to insert the gigantic epidural needle into my spine. I was never even willing to disrobe in a locker room, yet there I was, expected to be comfortable naked in front of everyone.

Next they laid me down and strapped me to what appeared to be a cross, of all things, arms outstretched. Finally, Dr. Lee came in, checking to see if the epidural had taken yet, and asked me to wiggle my toes. I did, but he touched the scalpel to me anyway. I flinched violently, and Dr. Lee then ordered the anesthesiologist to put me under. The last thing I remember was hearing him tell the doctor, "It's okay, I only lost her for a moment."

I woke up alone in the recovery room, crying. Where is my baby?

I was greeted by Big Nurse, "Oh, grow up, stop crying!"

"Where is my baby?" I demanded.

"They're going to bring her to you when you are back in your room," she replied without a hint of compassion. At last I could breathe a sigh of relief. I understood; she's alive!

When I was taken back to my room, I vehemently demanded that they bring my child to me immediately. Mother tried to keep me cool but it was no use. When they finally brought her to me, I refused to let them take her away again. She would not be returning to the nursery. They would have to bring the clear plastic crib into my room where she would rest with me, and at night when I was sleeping, to be sure they could not take her from me, I parked her in my bed right next to me.

Jessi was presented to me all wrapped up tightly in a blanket. I held my precious angel close to me and prayed to remember this tender moment. Then I carefully unwrapped her as my mother watched. I took the mittens off her little hands, wanting to be sure she had all ten fingers and ten toes. And there she was, completely perfect and so beautiful. She had a full head of thick, midnight-black hair and a little at her ankles as well, but they assured me that it would go away soon. It wouldn't have mattered to me if it didn't. Later in life, she would occasionally good-naturedly complain about my choice of such a furry father.

I named her Jessica, which in Hebrew is Ishiah. I liked the exotic sound of it and the fact that I'd never known a girl named that, though it was used as a last name. As she grew up, this Hebrew version of her name never appealed to Jessi, and she refused to accept it.

Jessi's strong will was apparent the moment the mittens came off. Her individualism and sense of self showed itself early on. I felt I was there in the role of guardian rather than guide. There seemed to be something solid directing her from within. I knew intuitively that she needed to be treated gently and to be wrapped in love, made easy by her angelic presence.

When they handed me the birth certificate to fill out, I gave her my last name to avoid the inevitable questions that different last names would bring. Unfortunately, I would then be referred to as Mrs., which I was not. Then there was the line declaring the father's name, where I wrote, "Mother prefers not to state." I had waited two weeks after her birth to let Simon know that she was alive and well. He thanked me for calling him and said he was happy for me.

From the moment I presented Jessi to my wonderful mother, she held her as if she were the Holy Grail and fell instantly in love with her. I could almost see her heart leap out of her chest. This child, whose arrival she had been so concerned about, melted away all her fears. Jessi became her favorite grandchild, and they were as close as two peas in a pod.

I don't know what I would have done without my mother then. We would have had nowhere to go. She and I were not at all alike, but I would find myself one day wishing I was more like her. She was strong and had the brain of a businesswoman, but after her marriage, she had no chance to show it.

Jack came a day later. He was aware that there was a small doubt as to her paternity. When he took Jessi in his arms, he looked at her with the familiar wonder that first-time fathers often do. At that moment, I wanted him to be the one.

He seemed irresistibly drawn to Jessi, as if she pulled him from within. He wanted her to be his daughter and I did think he would be a good father because of his underlying tenderness. However, his intense resentment of me would stand in the way of our ever putting a normal family together.

I was four days in the hospital with my precious angel by my side. Dr. Lee suggested I might be able to leave on the third day, but I told him I was not ready, that I felt the incision was not yet closed enough. He kindly agreed. The truth was that I was afraid to take her home. The minute I left the hospital, the responsibility for her wellbeing would be all mine.

When the day came to take Jessi home, my mother's best friend Rita Bishop was there to help us. She herself had given birth to thirteen children and suffered two miscarriages. Her husband Larry had asked her to marry him on their second date when she said she wanted to have twelve children. To this day she insists she only said ten! We referred to her offspring as "the Bishop's dozen". Rita put Jessi into the car seat for me and drove us to Mother's, as I hysterically insisted she not drive over 25 mph.

I had made a small nursery for Jessi in the large vanity area off Mother's bedroom. There was a beautiful white cradle with a white eyelet sheet, pink ribbons, and ruffled fittings that I had made myself. There was also a small bookcase with 245 children's books I had carefully collected, including the complete Disney Children's Encyclopedia and a few cardboard beginner books. Once I heard Mother whispering over the phone to her sister, my Aunt Marion, "Do you believe she has 245 books waiting for the child?" I think she thought I'd slipped into some sort of eighth-month madness.

I laid Jessi gently in the cradle, totally in love. We had some difficulty with the breastfeeding at first. I had not properly prepared my nipples, because the idea of tugging on them as a way of toughening them seemed ridiculous to me. Also, Jessi had difficulty latching on, possibly due to the remaining influence of the anesthesia, but that would pass. Mother pressed little Jessi's head to my breast, and slowly we got started. Mom also gave her bedroom to us, taking my place on the sofa.

Jessi slept through the night without a peep. Dr. Lee told me I needed to wake her up to feed her. I set the alarm for 3:30, then I would gently pick her up, wrap her in my arms, and take her to my bed, where I would rest on one side and give her my breast. She hardly ever cried. She slept so quietly and so soundly, I would often go in to check on her, tickling her feet to see if she moved. Then she would jiggle a bit, and I'd let her be.

For the next two years I was with her day and night. I read to her constantly, afraid my dyslexia might have passed on to her. I did everything I could think of to help her. As soon as she could focus, I propped her up in the baby seat and started flash carding her with numbers and the letters of the alphabet, A, B, C, D, thinking, "Now even my child knows I am crazy." But she was extremely attentive and did not complain, though it did seem as if she was trying to speak from the moment she came out of the womb! There was telepathy between us, and I tried to accommodate her in any way I felt she needed or wanted.

When she learned to crawl, it was often over to a pile of books, which she would then drag across the floor to me, pulling herself up and slamming the book down on my knee, insisting I read it to her. I realized you can take the child out of Israel, but you cannot take the Israeli out of the child! Her personality was so sweet, it was clear she would grow up to be kind and loving. One of the many wonderful things she learned by crawling around was how to hide behind furniture, so that Grandma and I would come find her. Often, if I turned my back for just a moment, she would scoot away behind a recliner or the sofa. The first time she did, I screamed out to my mother, "I've lost the baby!"

We both began searching frantically, and I was nearly hysterical. When we finally found her, there was a delighted grin on her face. It soon became obvious she had found a new way to amuse herself. So Mother and I made a game of it. While Jessi was on the bed, we would accidentally pull the coverlet over her. Then I'd cry out to Grandma, "Where's the baby? Where's the baby!"

Mother and I would then pretend to search around the room a little, rustling through the blankets, and all the while Jessi remained still and silent. When we finally drew back the coverlet, she would burst into laughter, delighted to have tricked us again! Then we would laugh with her. She enjoyed her ability to make people laugh.

After just two months I found her with one arm poking out between the rails of her cradle. So from then on, she slept with me in the king-size bed with only one railing on her side to keep her from falling off. She never had a playpen because I did not want her to be contained. So Jessi was as free as a baby could be to learn, to discover herself, and very quickly she took herself in hand.

By six months old she pushed the spoon away as I tried to feed her and insisted on feeding herself. Sometimes she would feed herself too quickly and start choking, at which point I would hoist her out of the highchair, hold her upside down by her feet, and pat on her back until her throat cleared.

My brother Joseph loved Jessi. Her gentle manner and humor touched his heart. He was drawn to her sweetness despite the fact that he too was extremely angry with me. I had borrowed some money from him once to get back from Israel. I thought I had borrowed it from Mother. She didn't inform me she had taken it from Joe until I got home. I did pay him back, but in very small increments and over a long period of time. He was furious with me not only about that, but he disapproved of my choices in life.

I loved him and stood up for him all of his life. I asked my parents to put him in a special school. He needed help. I begged them to take him to a therapist, but by the time they realized he needed it, he was too old to be forced. Much of the time we lived with Mom, Joseph was in prison for having achieved his sixth DUI. Still, Mother remained devoted to him. He was her baby.

The first two years of Jessi's life, we were living off Medi-Cal, welfare, and food stamps. I never wanted her to realize how poor we were, so I surrounded her with rich things. She was always dressed beautifully. I taught her to enjoy the finer things in life, to want the best life had to offer in every sense, beginning with love. I ground her baby food fresh from what I cooked, and when she was a toddler we went to fine restaurants, where she would stroll around greeting people at each table, and if a baby was crying, she would run to comfort them.

Mother felt that we should be out on our own, and as frightened as I was to go, I eventually agreed. First, I would have to get a job. Cooper always said I would look good in the showroom, so I went to the largest furniture company in the area and was hired as a salesperson. I really enjoyed working in furniture and design. But trying to sell a client something beyond their means, I could not do. They kept me on for a year because I was good at customer service. Whenever there was a problem with a client or an order, they would call on me. My method was to get angrier than they were, which tended to have a calming effect. They believed me when I promised that I would solve the issue, and most of the time I did. But you can't get textile wrapped around your furniture if it is out of stock.

I found a small little cabin-like house in Covina for us. The front room had a bay window and a little dining room with a built-in hutch and bookcase. The kitchen was ample, and the only bedroom was small. I turned the empty laundry room into a small playroom for Jessi. I was able to furnish our tiny home with whatever I could find or get cheaply. I purchased a beautiful round antique table for under $35 and placed it in the bay window. It turned out to be a valuable antique. Jessi and I ate our meals there.

I was afraid of new places, with all their strange sounds and creaking, so I asked Mother to come and spend the first few nights with us, and despite the fact that she found it silly, she indulged me. Mother also agreed to take care of Jessi three days a week while I worked. I told her that corporal punishment of any sort was out of the question, and though she believed that an occasional swat on the diaper could do no harm, she begrudgingly agreed to follow my stipulations.

"Let's try something new this time," I quipped.

On the other two days, Jessi went to preschool. I scrupulously searched for the best nursery possible. I would make appointments with various nurseries and then show up a few hours earlier to catch them off guard. It's shocking the condition that children are kept in at some of these places. Once I walked in unexpected and discovered a woman had three babies strapped into high chairs in the kitchen, all screaming, crying and being ignored, while the other children played very quietly in her dirty little backyard.

Finally, I found Temple Shalom preschool. The sand-filled playground was in view of the classrooms. The children were taught the alphabet, numbers, and colors, among other things. The teachers were very kind. She would learn and be gently guided by Jewish hands. On Fridays they would say the blessings over challah and grape juice, visit the Temple, and learn songs. I took Jessi to see the place before agreeing to place her there, because I knew it had to be her decision, too. She seemed a little apprehensive at first. The teachers assured me that it could take a couple days, but she would be fine.

Those same teachers looked at me like the mother of Godzilla on the second day when I brought Jessi back to the school. She had hit and bit several of the children on her first day there. She was unaccustomed to playing with children other than her cousins. I was surprised but I maintained my cool and reminded them that they themselves had told me it could take a couple days for her to adjust. So they did allow her to stay and there were no further incidents of that sort.

I did notice two girls bullying her on the playground one day when I came to pick her up. How quickly the idea of corporal punishment flashes through one's thoughts. The desire to protect and defend my daughter in every instance was very powerful. Normally when I came to pick her up, she would be sitting with one of two boys: the blond-haired angelic one and the dark-haired bad boy. Unlike her mother, she was drawn to the light sweet one, and they would soon be seen holding hands, becoming very close friends for many years. Jessi was usually only in school for the morning or until early afternoon. I picked her up as early as I could, always anxious to see her. She would run into my arms.

I was vacuuming while Jessi, 22 months old, sat on the floor with a large new hardbound copy of Beauty and the

Beast. Though it was not a child's picture book, I noticed she seemed to be reciting what was printed on the pages as she turned them. I thought to myself, "Ah, she has a good memory like her mother." Then I realized I had only read that to her once, maybe twice, but thought nothing more of it. Interesting the impressions we skip over without understanding what's actually going on.

Then one day when I popped in to pick up Jessi at my mother's, she greeted me saying, "Well, you'll never believe what she did today!"

My thought was something like, Oh God, what crystal hit the floor? A bit too weary for a guessing game I asked, "What did she do?"

"She read me the newspaper!"

"Mother, please!"

Annoyed that I had difficulty believing it, she spoke through her teeth, "I am telling you she picked up this paper, pointed to the advertisements and said, 'Oh look Grandma, deodorant. Look Grandma, detergent, antiperspirant.'"

I sunk down onto one of the kitchen chairs. Was I thrilled? Not as much as I was concerned, though I was careful not to show it. I had known so many brilliant people whose genius had not always worked in their favor. Jessi was just about to turn two and yet she could read! Turns out the fortitude of her heart would hold her high above the entrapment of her intellect.

Meanwhile, thinking perhaps she could use a tutor to help her learn to read, I found a teacher willing to work with her. But Jessi spent the entire hour crawling around under the coffee table. After the second session the woman explained to me, "I cannot teach her. She has cracked the language code. It's like when Mozart approached the piano at three and just began to play. No one knows how they do it, it just happens."

More profound for me were the many unusual things Jessi began saying around three years of age. Especially of note was the occasional declaration, "You remember, Mother, when I was in Israel, but I was big."

It startled me the first time she said it, but I shrugged it off as just an odd comment. Then she said it again sometime later and then at least once more until it was clear to me that this soul who had asked entrance through me wanted me to know it was here with me now. I have treasured this secret and all it means to me, that there is no power greater than love, and that love never dies.

Then there was the time Jessi was sitting propped up against the pillows of our well-made bed when she called for me to come. I sat down beside her.

"Mother, I need you to help me with the puzzle."

"What puzzle?"

"The puzzle, the puzzle," she repeated, a bit agitated. Then as if there was a puzzle in her lap, she said, "There is a piece missing, and I need you to help me find it."

Before I could respond she added, "You know, Mother, sometimes you just take the love and throw it in the garbage!"

I was so stunned I didn't know what to say.

By the time Jessi reached four she had long been teaching herself to write. Being that I am left-handed and she is right-handed, I felt unable to help her properly. So the idea came to enroll her in school early. I was also under the belief that finishing high school at 16 would be desirable. I decided to ask if they would admit her into the local Montessori School. The director attempted to explain to me that she was nine months too young for their program. I convinced her to just meet Jessi, interview her, and then decide.

When I took Jessi in for the meeting, we were led into the empty upper-grade classroom, where Jessi pointed to the pictures of the planets posted above the blackboard, "Oh, look Mommy, there's Uranus and Pluto and Saturn and...."

The interview was over before it began. The director threw her hands up in the air and said, "Okay, we'll take her. Just lie about her age on the application."

Adjusting to kindergarten even at Montessori was a little challenging for Jessi. She wasn't used to being directed or told what to do. I had actually raised her according to a theory from B.F. Skinner's Walden Two that children should not be raised on a rigid schedule, the idea being that they should be allowed to eat when they were hungry and sleep when they were tired. This made the enforced naptime difficult at best, and getting her to sit with the other children during circle time was a bit of a chore. But once she got used to it, I asked the teacher how it was going, and she said, "Oh, it's okay now, she sits with the others in circle and shares. The only problem is that none of the other children understand what she is talking about!"

As I look over these words now, I realize they do not come close to describing what having Jessi meant to me and for me from the beginning. First and foremost, her precious existence proved to me that Love is eternal and unstoppable. Whoever it was that had called upon me from within was here with me again, and together we would each exalt our own lives.

It was the definitive end to my drug abuse. Oh, I would continue to smoke pot and cigarettes for a long time to come, but the days of snorting and basing cocaine were well over. I took my responsibility as the parent of this precious child more seriously than I'd ever taken anything in my life. No question that I would lay down my life for her. Almost any mother understands this. However, in our particular case, it was she who saved mine!

I was fascinated watching my little child grow up. It was as if I were given the chance in some way to see myself grow up again. Interesting how children are born with their personalities already intact while the character develops, and then seeing the familiar traits manifest. Like David, Jessi could not bear the seam in socks because it troubled her toes.

I saw her love of music develop. She began to sing as soon as she could talk and that began unusually early. One morning when she was just two, I heard her singing "Under the Sea" in the same tone and Jamaican accent of Sebastian the Crab from The Little Mermaid. I went quietly into our bedroom and momentarily banged my head against the wall. I was just a little concerned realizing that the actor had also now arrived.

She was gifted with a beautiful voice. That she came by honestly, as many in my family were good singers, and a few were extraordinary. My father won the national Paul Whitman Award for his singing when he was 15 and remained famous in his hometown of Buffalo. I too have a good voice, so singing together became part of our fun. When we were at the market shopping for groceries, we would sometimes sing and dance up and down the frozen food aisle. Perhaps that's why she eventually developed a love of musical theater, which she would later introduce me to, as I had missed it along the way in my parochial theater studies.

Then long before I even imagined she was ready to be introduced to John Coltrane, she made a comprehensive study of the history of jazz, and by the time she was 18 she would teach herself to sing jazz standards with the depth of a 40-year-old woman. She would be welcomed and appreciated in the local jazz clubs by astounded audiences. Nonetheless, she would choose not to become a singer professionally. She did not want to be chased by fans in the street.

For now, in these ever-precious moments, days and years, she was my little girl to love, to watch over, and to care for. Beyond that, she was truly and clearly guided by herself alone.

Chapter Eighteen – Jessi 2

Jack was having a hard time reconstructing his life after finally escaping drug addiction. Eventually, he recovered his stability as a writer in the film industry and was a large part of our support system. He visited us twice a week. He really enjoyed holding Jessi in his arms, and once she started crawling, he enjoyed playing with her. It annoyed me however when he talked baby talk to her, and it annoyed him that I didn't allow him to change her diapers. In part, I couldn't understand why he'd want to. Beyond that, I was hyper-vigilant to protect her modesty.

Each time he came to visit we shared a meal together. Either he would take us out or I'd make dinner for us, knowing how Jack enjoyed my cooking. He always brought something for Jessi—a book, a toy, or perhaps a lovely dress. Often, he planned outings for us to take her on together. Otherwise, he would sit and play with her, either on the living room floor or in his car that they pretended was some kind of fantastic traveling machine. Jessi found him funny. He knew how to amuse her and his intelligence was more than enough to keep her interested. It was clear that he wished with all his heart that she would turn out to be his. It was also clear that it would not matter in the end, as he had come to love her. It must've been Jessi's love for each of us that kept us together in this family-like construct. But Jack still had a very hard time masking his complete contempt for me.

Jessi wasn't yet a year old, barely a toddler, but I always loved July 4th and wanted her to see the fireworks. We stopped at KFC and picked up a yummy meal. Jack took her on a few gentle rides and helped me with her on the carousel, guarding us as I held her tight upon the horse. Then we headed to the outskirts of the crowded grounds, laid a big blanket down, and set up the picnic. As night fell, Jessi laid on the blanket with a pillow under her head, watching the fireworks, calling out "Kaboom!" with each new explosion. I remember that day as a particularly happy one.

When Jessi was nearly four, Jack and I took her to Disneyland. As we entered the grand gates, she seemed all at once amazed and apprehensive. This sudden change of worlds, each unraveling into another, was a bit overwhelming. And giant strangers dressed up as cartoon characters posing for pictures was not quite her thing either.

We all stood in line for Space Mountain for over an hour, only to be told at the end that she was just a bit too short. We were led out the exit doors where I noticed the handicapped entered. Jack was about to walk on to another ride when I stopped him. "No way!" I said, pulling Jessi towards me.

I put a bulky jacket on her and brushed her hair up into a high ponytail. Then I walked us up to the handicapped entrance where I explained that I have severe claustrophobia and couldn't wait in a crowded queue. Truthfully, this had long plagued me. Standing enclosed by strangers is unbearable for me. I can feel what they are feeling, all of them at once, unless I zero in on one particular individual's feeling and then another's. The theatre training had made me hypersensitive to the energy of emotions, and that combined with claustrophobia was increasingly agonizing as the minutes and sometimes hours dragged on. I would tell myself, 'Buck up, you can take it, no one else is bothered by this', but that day I said no. We got through to the ride, no one noticed she was a bit too short, and it was the last time we stood in line!

Jack was constantly vigilant of Jessi, which was the good news. I knew he would throw himself in front of a moving train to protect her, if need be. So what troubled me? The growing possessiveness and demands for private time to develop his own, separate relationship with her somehow made me cringe. No, I was not anxious for him to be alone with her. He was always able to relate well with little children. Perhaps it was their simple innocence that attracted him; perhaps it made him feel strong?

When Jessi was two, we agreed to run a blood test to see if Jack was in fact the father. Jessi wasn't so good with needles, but Jack was worse, and he could faint at the sight of a needle. After the lab we went to the Queen Mary in Long Beach for a stroll around the docks and had lunch at Winston's. There was a Louisiana jazz band playing, and Jessi stopped to dance for them, much like Shirley Temple, curls and all. As we sat enjoying a delicious, formally served lunch, Jack looked straight in my eyes and said, "I want you to hear this. It doesn't matter how it turns out. I love her like my own, and I am not going anywhere!"

I believed him, though even now it is difficult to understand the growing acrimony and passive aggression that seethed out of him towards me continuously. He was determined to take ownership of Jessi in some solid way, even offering to adopt her. I suggested we wait until she was older and let her decide. That infuriated him even more; he was at least fulfilling the Disneyland Dad role.

However, if we were driving and Jessi started crying in her car seat, as children sometimes do, Jack would become agitated, pulling over to the side of the road or into the nearest parking lot. He'd get out of the car screaming, slam the door, and demand that I make her stop crying before we continued on. He wanted a Disneyland doll.

When it came down to the real commitment, the caring and maintenance required of true parenting, he was not there. He was not there for the long sleepless nights that come with the beloved child's fever, the day-to-day struggle balancing the role of a mother and a father, or the constant measuring of one's self in the face of the growing child needing gentle guidance and enthusiastic attention. And God knows, my temperament failed me all too often.

Life in sales was short lived. I was just not good at it. I began to consider other avenues to work during the hours of Jessi's school, so that I might remain present in her life. Jack, knowing I had long practiced as a Chi Master, suggested I become a massage therapist, that he had heard it was one of the up-and-coming careers of the next century, and as it turned out, he was right. I didn't jump at the chance though. I gave it some thought and prayed, asking how could I start charging for something I had done so long for free. I finally heard the answer, "Charge for the massage, Chi free!"

I made a list of ten steps I needed to take to secure this new career. I went to my mother for a loan. She came through for us, as difficult as it was for her on a practical level. I realized we would have to move to the San Fernando Valley to reach a clientele rich enough to afford massage. I found the best Massage Therapy School in Encino and a small three-bedroom house, with one bath, wood floors, a fireplace, and a large, private backyard.

Jessi picked a brilliant blue for her room to be painted. It looked as if you were standing in a pool. Her pretty daybed and canopy were princess-like, and white lace curtains draped the windows. I remember going into that room one day and finding her with a blissful look on her face. She smiled and said, "Oh Mama, when I close my eyes, I see a golden moon in my head!"

I threw my arms around her and gave her a gentle hug. "Of course, you do, Darling!"

On the day we moved in, Jack and I put up Jessi's little playschool cabin at the end of the yard. Patty and Eli lived nearby with their three children, two boys, and a little girl named Candy. Jack despised Patty with a passion, he said it was because of the miserable way she sometimes treated me and, I realize now, my daughter as well. She never had a kind word to say about Jessi. I let it go unnoticed. I wish I had not. It would be some time before I would realize the need to let go of them all.

Jessi and Candy grew up together. They got on well together, though they were as different from one another as Patty and I. Their playtime together was divided between our two homes, except when it came to sleepovers. I refused to let Jessi sleep there, but I could not tell her why. It was because Eli was in the habit of coming home in the wee hours of the morning with cocaine and a couple of friends who would hover around the coffee table drawing out and snorting lines of cocaine until dawn.

Candy often slept over at our place. I had the impression that she was happier when she was in our home. One morning at the breakfast table, the subject of the gift came up.

Candy asked Jessi, "What is the 'gift'?"

"I don't know," she said. "I only know when my mother practices, her heart flies."

Jessi seemed to know and understand things she had no reason to know or understand. Not yet five years old, she became fond of declaring on any given occasion, "Oh Mommy, I already know about that; they taught us that in the sun."

I took the recurring comment in stride until she seemed so matter of fact I decided to ask. "Jessi, when you say you learned about that in the sun, what do you mean?"

"The sun, the sun, Mother! The place I was before I came to you."

"How did you get there?"

"I don't remember. I only know I was very sick when I arrived but they took care of me until it was time to come to you."

"Who took care of you?"

"The angels!"

"How did you come to me?"

"They led me down a pink tunnel, and I picked."

"Picked what?"

"You!"

***

I began my studies at the Touch Therapy Institute under the direction of a nurse named Maria with an MA in Kinesiology. She insisted on a comprehensive approach to the study of massage including rudimentary courses in biology, osteopathy, kinesiology, acupressure, and knowing every muscle of the body—its name, origin, insertion, and function.

I remember asking her at our initial meeting whether or not it was necessary for me to get a massage in order to be able to give it. She said while I studied in her institute I would both be taking massage and giving massage as part of my training. The idea of laying passive on a table while someone touches me would never be my thing, but I would have to submit to it in order to learn what it might be like for others.

The first few massages left me completely debilitated, like a house of cards having fallen upon itself. So I got used to offering to give the massage first.

When I went home, I would study for about an hour. Afterwards I would pick up Jessi at school and spend as much time with her as possible until she fell asleep. Then I would continue to study. I thought it would be easy to blend the massage with the Chi Gung, but not so. Eventually, I got the hang of it, and the use of Chi Gung would be the outstanding feature of my work, setting me well apart from the others.

An acupuncturist hired me the day I became certified as a massage therapist. I worked from 8:30 am until 5 pm without a break, my choice. I was fascinated by how much I was learning, more and more all the time. I saw 15 patients a day, working through lunch, taking only occasional cigarette breaks on the rooftop. I was able to give his patients great relief, and often they would just say they didn't need him after seeing me. Every patient got the best care I could offer, no matter how long it took; everyone else, including the doctor, could wait. The doctor then decided that the patients should see him first, then me. Some then booked only with me.

The doctor was an observant Orthodox Jew, and I enjoyed seeing his eyes light up when he spoke about the Messiah. Everyone means the same thing by that term; they just can't agree on whom. He lorded the Law over his Jewish patients, especially the women, reminding them to light the Shabbat candles and keep the faith in the house. I remember one woman answered his question as to whether she kept kosher, saying that her household was kosher but that they did not keep kosher when they ate out, to which the doctor responded, "So your house will go to heaven, and you will go to hell!"

We actually had miraculous success combining our expertise to save countless patients from their injuries, pain, and disease. Unfortunately, the doctor could not stand the competition. He had his office manager tamper with my time card and then accused me of doing it. I couldn't believe he would sink so low, but he did.

Jack and Jessi came to pick me up from the office that day. I don't remember why. Perhaps my car was in the shop. In any case, I tried to hide from Jessi that her Mama was in tears, afraid because so much depended on me. Then, on the way home, I saw a large chiropractic office on the same street and asked Jack to stop a minute while I ran in. I informed Dr. Robert that he needed a new massage therapist and that I was the one. I told him I would come back the next day and give him a massage. He hired me immediately afterwards.

It was there that I met Nadera or Nadi, as she called herself. She was, without question, one of the most intelligent women I've ever known. She always presented herself as a ten. Her thick hair was perfectly coiffed, shoes and clothes were designer only and kept like new. Nadi was beautiful, sexy, and stacked; her décolletage was proudly visible between the lapels of her white doctor's coat.

She had studied medicine in Asia, then for reasons I do not know, went on to chiropractic college from there instead of taking the medical boards. It was there that she met Robert, and she helped him through his studies. When they graduated they went into business together. Both Nadi and Robert loved my massage. They respected me as a Chi Master, marveling at the energy that poured through my hands. I was their only massage therapist, and with their help became the most sought-after massage therapist in the rather expansive Persian community of the Valley.

Nadera was married to a contractor. She bore him four children. After the birth of her last child, she left the hospital early and went home unexpectedly. Playing back the phone messages, she discovered that her best friend was calling to leave a message for her husband.

Alarmed, she went to the housekeeper and asked, "Does she often call here to speak with my husband?"

The housekeeper blanched white. When Nadi's husband returned home that night, she told him she had him on videotape screwing her best friend in their very own bed. Of course, she did not really have any such evidence, but he confessed outright. For this, she forced him to sell their Malibu mansion and moved the family to Calabasas.

Nadi had asked me if I knew of a good psychiatrist, explaining that she was asking for a friend, and as the friend was Persian, it couldn't be another Persian because of the rapid manner in which gossip spreads throughout their community. I had no idea at the time that she might have been asking for herself. She had not gotten over the betrayal of her husband and trusted friend, nor would she ever. The old conditioning from Persian society made women believe that they had no identity without a man, however brilliant and educated they might well be, even beyond their husbands. Alone meant unwanted and unfit.

She was still quietly seething when I met her, though she hid it well. She expressed some interest in the peace that my Teacher was offering and told me she wept when she first listened to the cassette of his I gave her. Then she decided to get her MD not only for the accomplishment but for the money. The plan was for her husband to care for the children until she finished her residency and then she would take the children away from him and finish raising them independently. She studied for six months and passed part one of medical boards. Then she went on with study groups, and after another year, passed the final exams. Her specialty was in pain management, though sadly she would not succeed managing her own pain. She was hired at Kaiser immediately after completing her residency.

Later, she called asking if I was still involved with my Teacher. She wanted me to know that I had always been very special to her and that she truly appreciated our friendship. I told her that she was very dear to me, too.

"Let's meet for lunch," I said. "Just name the time and place."

"Sure." She said she'd let me know. But after I hung up, I had a strange feeling. Why hadn't we made the appointment for lunch right then and there? Two weeks later Robert called, asking if I had heard from Nadi.

I told him yes, just recently. There were a few beats of emptiness. "What is it Robert?"

"She's dead."

"Come on!" I said, thinking he must be playing some trick on me.

"No really, I am telling you, she killed herself," he whispered desperately into the phone.

"Why?" (always the first question and never really answered). "What happened?"

"She had become addicted to Xanax. She was getting it from hospital supply. (Meaning no doctor was supervising her self-medicating.) She left a note saying, 'This is because of my husband.'"

So that phone call she made to me was her goodbye. I was furious with her. It was my birthday and I had just come from cremating the remains of my baby brother Joseph. He was hit by a car as he attempted to cross the street in a wheelchair. I wasn't in the house five minutes when Robert called with the tragic news, and my sorrow was compounded. I had always respected and loved her dearly.

***

I lied to my daughter twice. I think my mother might have considered them "white lies" as they are often used to shield someone from a hurtful or emotionally-damaging truth. First, I let her believe that her father and I had been married. I wanted to protect her from society's glare. I continued to lie by omission until she asked me a direct question, "What did you wear?"

I told her I had worn the dress I always wanted to—a beautiful white sari laden with gold. I don't think she ever asked for pictures, but if she had, I would've simply told her I did not have them, which would be true. I would tell her the truth only when I had to.

Then there was the lie about my education. I told Jessi I had a Master's degree in Theater. To my accounting, I truly had more than the equivalency of whatever was needed for that degree. But there was no piece of paper handed out by either Ossetynski after five years or Grotowski's Theater Laboratory. I told her I attended UCLA, so the logical conclusion would be that I received a Master's in Theater from UCLA.

The truth is, I never got any degree beyond my high school diploma and I was never enrolled as a student at UCLA, though I did live in Westwood and audited classes there frequently. But it was always by my own choice, in my own time, and for my own reasons. I was not in any way prepared to dance to the beat of so many other drums. I went my own way, and until this day, I do not regret it. But I wanted my daughter to have the benefit of a degree, because I had later suffered from the lack of it. So I led her to believe that I had it, thinking if she knew that I did not, she would not get one either.

There is an unsupported theory about the adoptive-child syndrome, which includes lying as a way of getting by or being accepted, more prevalent in those adopted at a later age as Jack was, at four years. The adoptive parents had changed his name entirely, the first and the last. Naturally, it was not beneath him to tell big lies while interviewing for a writing job in the industry. Once he told them he had been a fighter pilot in Vietnam. Actually, he was in Boot Camp for only a couple of weeks before he was discharged. Jack also suffered from acrophobia. He did get the job. It involved going down to New Zealand. They decided that, as a fighter pilot, he would enjoy a brisk flight through the fjords. Jack wore sunglasses so that the pilot could not see that he had his eyes closed. When they finally landed, he got out of the plane and threw up all over himself, passing it off as food poisoning.

I've always been good at detecting a lie. I assume it's because of the intensive work I did in theater that taught me to listen, to see, to feel, and to recognize body language, as well as sense the vibration of energy in the air. But knowing someone is lying is useless unless you can prove it or get them to admit it.

The acrimony between Jack and I continued to grow. He felt that the money he was contributing to our welfare should earn him the full rights of a father. More and more he was demanding private time with Jessi. He wanted to take her on a camping trip for several days because a friend of his had done that with his daughter. I refused to allow it saying, "Let's all go together." I was okay with us all hanging out together. I thought it would give Jessi a feeling of some kind of family. And I was okay with Jack taking her on short trips to the store or even to an occasional movie.

Then he would say something like, "A friend of mine got us tickets to the Dodgers game."

"Great, I'd love to go."

"It's not for you!"

More and more often he would make derogatory comments about me in front of my daughter. Occasionally, he would threaten to withdraw his support if he couldn't at least spend the night alone with her at his place. I told him he could do whatever he liked, but that was not going to happen. I don't know if he thought that one day I would change my mind or that he could somehow muscle me into allowing it, but from my side, it was never going to happen.

Jack had learned the value of sucking up in the film industry, so we took the Montessori School's director and her husband out for dinner. I suggested we go to Tempo, an Israeli restaurant with amazing cuisine. There I noticed a man sitting not far from us at a banquet table with extended family members. He was wearing a yellow sweater with a collared shirt underneath. Gray-haired and very stately looking, he looked like a professor from the Hebrew University. He caught my eye as I passed their table on my way to the ladies' room.

I felt him when I crossed back by the table, purposely walking behind him. Throughout the dinner we were aware of one another. He occasionally looked over his shoulder at me, and I watched him as well. It is interesting how powerful attraction can be, though neither of us made a definitive move. I had not been with any man since I left Israel more than five years before.

Then suddenly a member of his family, his niece I think, got up from their table and walked casually over to me, smiling as she slipped a note into my hand. That is exactly the kind of thing that I would do, and I must say I truly appreciated it. I opened the note under the table, and it read "Shlomo Cohen" and a phone number. Then I wrote my name and phone number on a cocktail napkin and folded it over, placing it beside my plate.

When his family was leaving, Shlomo got up, walked over to me, and offered me his hand. I took it, placing the napkin in it, as I stood up and kissed him on both cheeks. He was tall and thin and wonderfully dignified. He glanced at the napkin and whispered in my ear, "I'll call you."

When I sat down, Jack flashed me a look. There was nothing going on between us romantically, and it seemed quite certain there never would be again. I was wildly attracted to Shlomo, and he was the first man who had caught my eye since Jessi was born.

For our first date, I sent Jessi away for the night, a rare exception to my rule against sleepovers. I can still see his wonderful face as if he was sitting across from me. Shlomo took me out for dinner at my favorite French restaurant, Moustache Cafe. We sat talking for hours, gazing into one another's eyes, so aware of the longing. We briefly filled each other in on our lives.

Shlomo was a structural engineer who owned his own company specializing in ironwork, with 36 employees. He designed and built balconies, railings, and even a two-story exterior staircase, for which the lady of the house was unwilling to pay the final fees. So Shlomo went over to her house the next day with the workmen and an electric power saw.

He stood there in front of the woman and told his worker, "Cut it down! Cut the whole thing down to the ground!"

The woman started screaming. She paid him immediately.

His ex-wife and his children were in Israel. He was ready to retire or at least to let go of this company. He wanted to return to Israel, to his children and his grandchildren, and put his family back together, so he was in the process of wrapping up his affairs here. He sought out and found jobs for every one of his 36 employees, with a raise. He was a clever, honorable man who had come from slim beginnings and made himself wealthy. He had been a soldier, and of his time there he said, "I know every corner of Israel, like a woman."

And yes, he knew what to do with a woman, every corner. It was the first time I made love on my own bed, in my own house, since Jessi was born. I did not have time to date nor would I have brought a man home to my bed with Jessi in the house. He was a magnificent lover. We were absolutely perfect together. It was as if we had been making love for years and years. I know that he felt it, too. It surprised us both.

But we would have very little time together, though he would string it out as long as he could. Sometimes we made love at his place in the middle of the day before I picked Jessi up from school. Any little time we could fit in was well worth the ecstasy. We would enjoy the precious moments we had. There was never any plan of me returning to Israel on his arm. He had already established in his mind his reason for returning and exactly how he would do it.

David was still waiting for me to return to him and his father. I could not break his heart again. So I asked Mother to come a few days before Thanksgiving to give me a little more time with Shlomo.

I invited him to the Thanksgiving feast, as well as Jack, who was absolutely convinced that Shlomo was with Mossad. He was the first to leave, and I wanted to follow after him, but my mother vehemently objected to me leaving the house on Thanksgiving evening, even after all the guests had left. So I went to see Shlomo the next night, which would be our last. He was leaving the following morning.

I arrived at his home that evening in a long black velvet swing coat wearing nothing but a tiny teddy underneath. I dropped the coat to my feet as I entered the room full of boxes. He swept me into his arms and made love to me with everything inside his heart. I heard him cry out, "It isn't fair." And I knew exactly what he meant. But I will always be grateful to him for opening the grave of my heart!

***

When Jessi was barely six, as she was sitting at the kitchen table, she called for my attention. She seemed very serious.

"Mother, I need to tell you something."

"What is it, baby?"

"I'm afraid someone is going to try to hurt me," she announced almost cautiously.

"Jessi, what do you mean?"

"I don't know," she said. "It's just a feeling."

"Well, who do you think is going to try to hurt you?"

She cast her eyes down to the floor, shaking her head gently.

"Do you think I'm going to hurt you?"

"No."

"Do you think Grandma's going to hurt you?"

"No, Mama," she said, as if of course not.

"Then who?"

"I don't know, Mom. I'm just afraid."

I dropped to my knees and embraced her. "Don't worry, honey, I won't let anyone hurt you."

"Okay, Mommy." She held me tightly around my neck.

Would that I had kept the promise I made to her at that moment, but I did not. I seem to remember my mother being with us that evening, though not in the kitchen at that time. I discussed it with her soon thereafter. She passed it off as not serious, just a child saying things. This from the woman who had difficulty believing that her husband had abused me. I did not mention it to Jack immediately, though now I wish I had. I should've demanded that we get into therapy immediately but instead I gathered my thoughts and started to think about what to do.

Perhaps Jack felt something, a change in my attitude, I don't know. He certainly could have picked up on my increasing reserve. In response he started laying the pressure on thick. His new attempts to seize power may have been grounded in the fact that his mother had just died and he was about to inherit a large fortune. He was expecting $5 or $6 million, as his mother had invested in General Motors and Sears from the outset of those companies.

Jack's father had disinherited him entirely, so his mother felt she should make it up to him and left him her entire estate. It would be several months, even a year before he could get his hands on the money but it was coming, and perhaps he thought with that he could fight me for ownership of Jessi with everything he had. I do not know. I do know that he was clearly attempting to drive a wedge between my daughter and me. The constant stream of expensive presents for her, the snide comments about Mommy, the "you and me". I felt the impending wealth was giving him a false sense of power. It was scary. I told Jack that he could no longer be part of our lives that he had to leave us alone, and so he did.

While still with the Orthodox acupuncturist, I had taken a job at a woman's gym and spa a few days a week. I continued to work there for the next 20 years. I doubled my work hours and redoubled my efforts to get private clients, because that's where the money was. I surrendered myself to unscrupulous doctors who were charging outrageous amounts to the insurance companies while only paying me $20 an hour for the many patients that paraded through our home into my private office. I had to find a way for us to survive, and so I worked as hard and as much as I could, but I still wound up short at the end of each month having to ask my mother to help me. I just could not afford the rent that was increasing by hundreds every year.

I often caught myself while wrapping up a piece of leftover cake saying, "I'll take this with me to school." To work at the spa is what I meant. I said it so many times that I began to realize the truth in it. I was learning in my work every day, with every patient. Every minute I spent with that patient I was learning about the body, about feelings, about the body's feelings and its locked-in memories, about people's thoughts, about how thoughts affect the body, and so on.

I am grateful to every one of them for allowing me to learn from them, for allowing me to treat them, to take care of them, to heal them, and to listen to their stories, where I learned about other worlds and the human beings within them. I give special thanks to the ones who would say, "I am praying for your hands." I was honored by their gratitude. Dr. Robert's mother told me, "You are the doctor!" I was highly complimented, as I also respected and loved her.

Jessi was in camp when I went to spend a couple of nights with my sister, Kate. Knowing all that had happened when I sent Jack away, she popped a cassette into the car tape player while driving me around on that particular visit.

"I want you to listen to this. It's called *Why People Don't Heal* by Caroline Myss PhD. She is a great medical intuitive. Just listen."

On some level I have always trusted Kate and so I took her suggestions to heart. I attempted to listen, all the while nodding my head. "Yeah, yeah. I know. I know this, I already know this." I wasn't listening in a way that I could put together what she was really saying, but Kate gave me the cassettes to take home, and a year later I started to listen to them. First, I understood that the term "medical intuitive" described part of what I do. Then I began to understand the importance of forgiveness, the danger of victimhood, and that I could divest myself of those robes.

For two months I listened to the two cassettes every time I was in the car. Myss theorized that relationships are examinations in and of themselves. And that even in a relationship that ends painfully, after much suffering, the person involved in that relationship with you would have had to at least loved you enough to act out that role for you, so that you could go through that examination.

If that were true, I theorized, then was it possible to bring actors back to play a different role, a different character or perhaps a new and improved version of themselves? Somehow it all made sense to me. Even my Teacher would say, "You forgive because you want peace."

***

Jack would be gone from our lives for almost seven years. There were two major catalysts that would predicate his return. The first was the passage through an examination. If one sees life as a continuous learning process, then in that lesson, thoughts, ideas, and beliefs are constantly changing and our understanding deepens. Mother never believed there was anything untoward about Jack. When she died, I sent a note informing him that she had passed. He sent a note back saying that he had always liked her, was sorry to hear that she was gone. There was no further exchange until several months later.

Once, I called Simon and asked him to pay for Jessi to attend a special performing arts camp in the summer between 6th and 7th grade with a friend. It was $250, the first and only money he would ever give. When he learned that mother had died, he asked me again to marry him. He said I would have to come to Israel for the wedding and to live, but that it would ensure that I would receive his Social Security in my older years. He asked me to think about it and talk with Jessi. I did ask her, and she flat out said, "No!"

She didn't want to go to Israel. She was just about to start performing with her school's musical theater group. She had her own life now, and it did not include immigrating to Israel. Simon was greatly disappointed. He finally decided to come and see us here. In the many times through the years we had discussed the idea of him coming, he offered to stay in a hotel. I would say, "No of course not, you will stay with us."

He would say, "No, I don't want to make a hurting. I will stay in a hotel."

But now he was pleading poverty again, and I began to understand that Simon was just expecting to come and move in with us, along with his now fully-grown son Yaad, who had been so brutally unkind to me when I was pregnant with Jessi.

No man had ever slept in our home while Jessi was there, and Simon was just a voice on the phone to her. She had never met him face to face. I was struggling desperately financially by now. I could not imagine what I was going to do with them sitting around the house all day while I went out and worked seven days a week. Also, I needed my car to get there. What would they drive? If I had learned nothing else in all my years of parenting, it was that my daughter needed to be protected—her feelings, her body, her space, and her world.

Simon sent Yaad ahead of him, a few days before. I don't know why, perhaps to scope the place out? I did not invite Yaad to stay with us. He stayed with friends he knew somewhere in Woodland Hills.

Jessi and I picked up Simon at Bradley International in Los Angeles. His eyes were rolling around in his head; he was so grateful to be on the ground again. I had often suspected that this brave tank soldier had a fear of flying but he always denied it vehemently. It sure looked like it at that moment.

He reached out to hug Jessi, and she did hug him back. Then he hugged me. It seemed odd that there wasn't that feeling that no time has passed. But here, now, it was quite different. So much time had passed, and my last moments in his presence had been miserable. And now I was looking at a man that I was no longer even remotely attracted to.

We walked to the parking lot, got in the car, and stopped at the pay gate. The lady asked for four dollars. I waited a moment for Simon to reach into his pocket and hand me the four dollars she was requesting, but nothing, not a move. When I had to reach into my wallet and pay, all the years of him giving nothing slammed into my head, and I began to seethe with anger, but I tried very hard to hide it. I had purposely not pursued him for child support, because in that case he could have demanded she visit him in Israel, and I was certain he would then do anything he could to keep her there.

When we finally got home, I showed Simon around the house and yard. I am sure he noticed that no bedroom has been set up for Yaad. I pointed out the spinach barakas I'd made for him and asked if he was hungry. He wasn't but asked if we could all just sit down together in the living room.

He had presents for us. For me it was a bottle of Versace perfume and a gold chain with a small Star of David medallion dangling from it. For Jessi he brought an array of clothes that had no chance of fitting her. Then he told her that he was going to help her get in shape.

I can't even imagine how disheartening that must have been for Jessi, who was struggling with her weight, and here comes her biological father with a handful of size 0 clothes. The one precious thing he did give her, she has never put on her finger nor does she want it. It is a ring made up of four precious diamonds that he designed, quite unique and beautiful, once promised to me. To this day, it sits in my jewelry box, never worn.

Jessi sat by herself in the big burgundy wingback chair, absenting herself from the conversation. He had come without any money after all these years, and here I was planning on asking him to stay in a hotel for a few nights so that Jessi could get used to him. I certainly didn't have the money to put him up in a hotel and he was shocked that I wanted him to.

I asked him if he could explain to Jessi why he had never sent any money for her support. He asked me to leave it for later, but I pursued. I am truly sorry for having opened that discussion with him in front of her at that moment. It was a vigorous attempt to push him away. To humiliate him like that in front of his daughter and to allow my daughter to see me humiliate him like that was very wrong of me. I thought I had finally gotten him to understand and agree that it would be better if he spent a few nights away and got to know Jessi gradually. But as he hopped in the car with Yaad's friend, I saw his eyes were full of tears. Jessi had refused to hug him goodbye.

He said to her, "I see you're like your mother. Okay, never mind."

I was all at once relieved and sad when he was driven away. I took Jessi to see the latest Harry Potter film in order to distract her from what had just happened. I was unable to enjoy a single moment of it because all I could think about was Simon and how terrible he must be feeling.

The next day Simon called. He was supposed to show up at a concert that Jessi's musical theater group was giving. She had learned a couple of songs in Hebrew especially for him. But he did not come; he never showed up. When I spoke with him on the phone he said, "No, leave it. I'm going back to New York."

I did everything but beg him to come. Begging was the one thing I had promised myself I would never do for him again. That day he cried was the very last time I saw him, and it cost me my relationship with my beloved David.

Two decades later I had a powerful dream about Simon. I had come back to Israel. David was still a boy and I held him in my arms all night long. Simon said I shouldn't leave because I had just gotten back. I felt him so near me and all that he was and I remembered why I loved him. I asked forgiveness for having taken Jessi from him and woke weeping.

Jessi sang her heart out at the Jewish Community Center that day. When we got home, Jessi sat so desolately on the sofa, my heart was breaking for her. I thought about Jack and how throughout the long absent years he had continued to send cards signed to Jessi, "I will always love you!"

I called him and asked if he still had room in his life for Jessi. He said that he was about to marry a woman he'd been living with for two years but that when he proposed to her, he stipulated if he ever had a chance to be part of Jessi's life again, she would come first. Nothing would stop him from returning to the child he truly loved.

When Jessi was grown I would ask her, "Do you resent me for bringing Jack back?"

"No, Mom, you did the right thing. I understand why you sent him away. You were scared. You made the best decision you could at the time, under the circumstances. And you were right to bring him back when you did. It showed me that you could forgive, and that despite your penchant for torching bridges, you were capable of rebuilding a few too. I am so proud of the enduring relationship that has survived between the two of you and I so admire the bond you've developed over the years. You're family. And that's beautiful."

Chapter Nineteen – Gary

By the time Jessi was nine, we had been on our own for almost three years, except for my mother, without whose financial help, I don't know what would have become of us. Despite the fact that I was working seven days a week, the company was somehow unaware of it for over six years. When they did finally discover it, they forced me to cut down to six days. Apparently, working seven is illegal.

I also had a beautiful office in our home and scheduled my private clients there in the hours when Jessi was home from school. I am proud that at least I was somewhere present in her life, though it meant that she would watch client after client walk in and out as she sat doing homework on our sofa, stranger after stranger getting a massage from her mother when she also needed one badly, as she had low back pain throughout her childhood. But it was rarely her turn.

It's complicated giving a massage to someone you love, because it is extremely difficult to remain objective. For this reason, surgeons are not permitted to perform surgery on family members. Emotion clouds judgment. With a client I knew immediately how much pressure they could take and where. If I discovered something on a stranger, I could analyze it properly, but if I found something, God forbid, on my daughter or my mother, I might not know what it was or even worse, miss it all together. On strangers, I was in complete control of my objectivity. If I found a lump, I could clearly see its color through my fingertips, so I could be fairly certain what it was. If it was a creamy color, I knew it was a lipoma and therefore benign. Unless it was near the spinal column, where the development of roots might strangulate the spinal stem, there was little to worry about. The client would check with their doctor at my request and return telling me I was right.

Occasionally I would find a dark lump that upon touching it sent intense sorrow up my arm, then I knew it was cancer. The client would become aware that I was examining something and ask, "What is it?"

I did my best not to alarm them, saying in the least charged way possible, "I want you to have your doctor check this. Okay?" Luckily, my clients did as I told them because they trusted me and respected my work. Unfortunately, I was always right about that, too.

I have never known of an acupuncturist who would work on a cancer patient, which is not saying that they do not exist, only that they all know it is very dangerous to infuse cancer with more energy, because it can easily cause it to spread. I, however, did not shy away from treating them. I was very careful how I used the energy and would sometimes have extraordinary success. One of my patients, Mona, came for her session one day and announced that she had just been diagnosed with stage 4 lung cancer, a peculiar type for non-smokers.

I took care of her. She scheduled appointments in tandem with her chemo. Then they discovered that it was actually ovarian cancer that had metastasized to the lungs.

They removed her ovaries, and she went into full remission. She was a fighter and she believed in me. Over the next seven years she remained my patient. She would go in and out of remission three times. When it came back for the fourth time, she was more worried about her husband than herself. He had already been through so much watching her struggle, she was concerned that he couldn't handle another round.

I discovered a mass in her abdomen. When she returned a week later, it had doubled in size. I asked her to go to Master Woo, the old Chinese Chi Master with whom I'd once studied some years back. She did what I asked without question. He worked with her and taught her some energy exercises she could do by herself. One such exercise involved imagining she was circulating the energy through her body while singing her favorite song, "Blue Skies." In the last two weeks she was full of bright light. You would have thought she was going to beat it again. I broke down completely when I got the call that she was gone. Only then did I realize how much I loved her. I went to her memorial service and spoke of her with such affection that everyone was weeping and wondered who I was. I had learned so much from her about courage and love. Now I realized how much love was the basis of the energy I used to help my patients. Mona, my dear, thank you with all my heart.

There were many extraordinary healings I was graced to be able to perform. Then there were those whom I could only make more comfortable as they died, like the beautiful teacher who came to me complaining of low back pain. I asked my standard questions. She lied. Then a week later she returned to me and said, "I wasn't completely honest with you the last time I was here." She paused, "I have bone cancer. I need your help."

Bone cancer is a very serious matter when taking massage, because the bones become brittle, and so the pressure must be very light. She mapped out a schedule for the next two months only. She told me she wanted me to be a part of her regime. Eventually I could only use "touch therapy" on her, hands over her body's aura rather than touching it. I was helping her stay in touch with her super body. As the calendar she set came to a close, the cancer invaded her brain and took her down fast. I would have to face another loss of someone I allowed myself to care about.

There were other successes that truly stunned even me. Like the Persian man in his 50s, who also had 4th stage lung cancer and was lying in the hospital with little expectation of surviving when his family called for me to come. I walked into his hospital room and saw his very aged father weeping copiously in the corner. I told everyone to get out, and before starting the treatment told the old man's wife to tell Grandpa he had to stop crying in the room. "No one should cry in his room or anywhere near it. If you must cry, go outside the hospital. Never let him see doubt in your eyes, and he will get out of here." How I came by that assurance, and even dared to say it, I don't know.

I gave him four treatments only. I knew my clients reached the maximum capacity for healing when my hands began to burn them. Two weeks after I first came to help him, he walked out of the hospital, alive, well, and in full remission.

One might think that with the talent I processed, I would have had a healthy income. But I undervalued my work so badly, possibly because I felt that I didn't really own it and was therefore reluctant to charge what it was worth until the last few years. So the financial struggles continued miserably. I drove really crummy cars that broke down constantly and cost a fortune to fix. I was still having trouble overcoming my father's all-too-Catholic admonition that, "Money is the root of all evil."

I took pride in my borderline poverty. There was a "holier than thou" attitude like I am so evolved I can be happy being poor. Of course, that overstates the desperation of our situation, but again, without my mother's help we would have lost our home long ago. She would ultimately give me almost everything she had. I supposed it was primarily because of Jessi. But one day she told me, "I helped you because you deserved it." My brothers never forgave me.

My attorney and his psychic wife invited us to their pre-Thanksgiving gratitude event. When the invitation arrived, I looked at it, shook my head, and with a heavy sigh, tacked it onto the refrigerator with a magnet. It was very unlike me to accept such invitations, but this one I knew I would, as if I was obliged to. I began planning what I would wear, though the event was two weeks away. It would be an emerald-green velvet, skin-tight, long-sleeved dress with a wide rouched yoke, wrapped well off my bare shoulders. I knew someone would be there waiting for me.

Jessi agreed to go with me. I remember being unusually nervous as I dressed for the evening. We arrived to find the house just beginning to warm up with delightful smells and welcomed friends. The wife was wearing a stunning peau de soie evening gown in chocolate brown. It clung to her amply curvaceous form as it draped to the ground. She greeted us warmly but made no immediate comment regarding the introduction I was somehow expecting. I wandered into the kitchen to see what they were up to. A sumptuous Thanksgiving feast was in the last stages of preparation. The scent of sage and spiced pumpkin filled the air.

Then Shane, their daughter, approached me cheerfully and asked if I was having a good time.

"Oh yes, but I think your mother is supposed to be introducing me to someone."

Shane burst out, "Oh let me do it. I'm psychic!"

"All right."

She thought for a moment. "Okay. How do you feel about grey hair?"

I shrugged my shoulders.

"Okay, I know who it is. It's Gary. Come on, I'll introduce you."

Shane introduced me saying many nice things very quickly all at once. But I don't think Gary heard her, because I noticed he couldn't take his warm brown eyes off me, as if entranced.

He invited me to sit down. Whoever he had been talking with faded into the background. I had his full attention. Gary asked poignant quirky questions, and I answered in a forthright manner. There was an easy, amusing banter between us. We covered the basics by the time dinner was announced. I jumped up, explaining that I should probably check on my daughter and outright declaring, "I'm hungry!"

Jessi rarely ate at parties. I wasn't sure why. I, on the other hand, would wolf down every meal at an embarrassing speed. Mother said I eat as if someone's about to take the food away from me. I think it's because, like my father, I want hot food to be hot. So I wanted to get to the food before it turned cold, as buffets often do. I filled up my plate and ate by myself in the backyard.

Jessi seemed anxious to go. Or was I rushing to escape? I did go looking for Gary before leaving. There he stood, his back to me, so tall, so strong. I tapped his shoulder, and as he turned to face me, I kissed his cheek to say goodbye. Then when we hugged, a warm sparkling energy emanated profusely between us. I think we were both a bit startled, looking at one another just a moment.

"May I call you?" he asked in such a gentlemanly manner.

"Sure."

"I'll get your number from Shane."

"Okay."

After bidding goodnight to our host and hostess, I walked with Jessi out of the party, quietly surprised to still be feeling the warmth of his embrace.

The sun was setting when Gary called two days later. I was pleased to hear from him, and we spoke with the same ease we had in our first meeting. He apologized for his hoarse voice.

I commented, "Jung's wife said that 90% of the woman's attraction to a man is his voice."

"How am I doing?"

"Let's hope you get well soon!"

"Ouch."

"I'm kidding. You're fine."

I knew he was smiling. We made a dinner date for that weekend. Gary let me choose the restaurant. I picked my favorite Israeli place.

I asked Mother to come take care of Jessi, whose response to his arrival was less than welcoming. When I attempted to apologize for her he said, "It's okay, she's just afraid that I'm going to take you away from her."

I triple-checked that I had locked the front door behind us, and he quietly commented on our way to the car, "If you tell yourself you are locking the door as you lock it, you will remember that you did." I tried that next time and it turned out he was right. One compulsive behavior overcome.

He had a slick red sports car with a black ragtop, but I couldn't tell the make and model in the dark, so I asked, "What kind of car is this?"

"Doesn't matter."

He didn't want me to care about what kind of car he drove, as if I would! It was in fact, a beautiful brand-new red Mustang convertible with a very loud engine.

He was nicely dressed in a crisp shirt with a parson's collar and a handsome jacket. I was wearing a beautiful cream-colored sweater, embellished with gold. My hair was curled and cascading over my shoulders.

Once we had ordered he looked at me across the table and said, "The moment I saw you walk into the room, I wanted to kiss you all over."

I was surprised that he would make such a revealing comment about his feelings at the very beginning of dinner. Even more interesting, he repeated it three times by the time we finished our first glass of wine and then added, "You must think it's strange that I keep repeating the same thing, but for me it was a very powerful moment when you walked in."

I confessed that I'd carried his embrace with me out the door that first night we met. We continued eating, and he watched with delight as I gobbled it down.

Gary was a nationally renowned psychologist. He and his ex-wife had been interviewed on "60 Minutes" because they were two psychologists living together for years though still unmarried, the trend of the times. He did marry her eight years later, and they stayed together for seven more. His parents, however, never knew that he had married her until he told them they were divorcing. Beyond that, he gave no more information regarding the cause of their divorce.

As we were leaving, it was the first time I noticed he had a small gray ponytail in back. I remember reaching out to touch it as he opened the car door for me and I said, "You don't need this anymore." Really? Who was I to tell him he didn't need that or anything else anymore? Either he didn't hear me or he was just being polite about it, as he made no remark. Anyway, I would eventually like the ponytail as well. It is funny, the audacious remarks that thoughtlessly fly out of my mouth sometimes.

When we arrived at my house, he wrapped me in his arms and kissed me passionately in the car. Had I been standing up, I would surely have melted to the floor. I was still woozy as I got out of the car. We said goodnight and not another word. I knew I would see him again because I could feel the hook in my heart.

It was several days before he called again. We chatted for a while, as always with tender and touching moments. Then he asked if I'd have dinner with him over the weekend.

"I have an idea," he said. "I'd like to invite you to dinner at my home."

"Really? What would you like me to cook?"

"I'm cooking!"

"Really? Excuse my surprise, but I've never had a man cook for me before."

"Tell you what, I'm going to be in the kitchen cooking and you're going to be sitting in the living room getting over yourself," he said, without a trace of malice.

"Okay."

"I'll pick you up at seven on Saturday, okay?"

"Sure," I said smoothly. "I'll see you then."

I hung up the phone and might've started dancing in the kitchen, if I had not already been pacing around wondering what to wear.

One of my Israeli girlfriends offered to let Jessi spend the night at her house. Her son was Jessi's age, and they got on well together. I knew my friend would watch over them and they would sleep in separate rooms.

I was so excited as I prepared for our date, I could hardly keep my hands from trembling to get my makeup on straight. Then there was the fact that I was still smoking cigarettes and pot. I didn't want him to know about either, so I put a plastic shower cap over the hot rollers in my hair and went outside to smoke my last few cigarettes before getting dressed. I was able to go 24, even 48 hours, without smoking a cigarette if necessary, my willpower was that strong.

But as soon as I returned home, I would smoke four or five at once to make up for lost time. My anxiety level gradually rose just until the moment Gary knocked on the door, and then suddenly I became extremely calm. The ravenous hunger I'd let gather throughout the day was also gone.

A broad smile shone across his face at first sight of me. He too was suddenly at ease. We hopped in the Mustang and off we went on the short jog across the freeway from Encino to Agoura. The roaring engine and the fact that he was somewhat deaf in his right ear made it very difficult for him to hear me, were it not for the voice training that allowed me to place my words on his heart.

He raced in and out of the first and second lanes, watching the surrounding traffic, as he stared out the windshield.

"I don't want to lose myself in another relationship only to have it end in screams and curses."

I was again surprised at his candor, though now I realize he'd had enough of the games and pretense. That remark from anyone else might have made me feel defensive, but I remained calm, and instead of arguing with him or trying to convince him otherwise, I told him a story.

It was about a young couple who meet and fall in love at a masquerade ball. Instead of removing their masks at midnight with the other guests, they decided to wait until dawn to take their masks off. But by dawn war had broken out, and the young man went off with the soldiers. Left behind, she did what women do while war goes on, waiting and hoping that one day he'd return to find her. When the war was over, the young man searched the four corners of the earth and never found her, having little more to go on than a masked woman. Finally, he settled on marrying a woman just to be married, but he left her bed cold, and she eventually died of a broken heart. As he packed up her things, he came across a box. He opened it, and there was the mask.

I felt Gary shudder. "Well, aren't you the storyteller."

I grinned and said, "Like Scheherazade." When we arrived at his condo, he poured us each a glass of white wine. We toasted to life; L'chaim. He took a perfect salmon fillet out of the refrigerator and laid it down on a piece of wood beside the vegetables that he had prepared for roasting on the grill. I asked if I could help and he told me I could go and sit down. I watched him cooking, intrigued. My fear of having to suffer through a bad meal was quickly fading. Gary explained, as I glanced around, that this small condo was merely a way station while he searched for a home to purchase.

I remember now, he complained about his neck hurting and the loss of mobility in it. I told him I could help him with that, and we talked about scheduling a massage for him at my home. Though I would not charge him, he would have to come as any other patient and leave immediately afterwards. He agreed, and we set a date.

The dinner was absolutely delicious. He roasted the vegetables to perfection. The salmon was mouthwatering, perfectly seasoned. He was a true chef. After we cleaned up the dishes together, he beckoned me to come and relax with him on the sofa. I must admit I was nervous. He suggested I lay my head down at the other end, picked up my feet, and began to massage them. I was impressed with his ability and allowed myself to accept it. Slowly, he would wrap me in his arms. Ever so slowly, he disrobed me entirely. Then he picked me up and carried me to his bed. He stripped naked before me, first exposing his gorgeous gigantic chest. Then he climbed in bed beside me and held me in his embrace as we fell asleep.

In the bright morning I hopped quickly into the bathroom to shower. I washed off the old makeup, only to paint it anew. My hair was a wreck so I washed and conditioned that too. It was a little remarkable how many shampoos and conditioners he had for a man with so little hair. Every available space was filled with many different varieties. It seemed to me like I was in there for a long time, so when I came out, I said, "I suppose you know why it took me so long."

"You couldn't decide which shampoo to use?"

I really enjoyed his sense of humor. We had some coffee and a quick bite to eat. Gary asked if I'd like to take a walk by the stream with him before he took me home. I said sure and followed along behind him as he led me down the path.

I think I must have asked him something about his ex because he made a quick derogatory comment about her, then nothing more. He was still in a lot of pain about whatever had happened between them, and he absolutely did not want to talk about it, though it had ended many years before. I did not press him.

Instead I enjoyed his presence, walking along beside him, our gait connecting rhythmically. We both barely dared to hope that this would work out but the pleasure of being together was seducing us. I felt closer to him with every step we took, though I was somewhat concerned that he had laid naked with me all night and not gotten hard once, nor attempted to make love to me. I put those thoughts aside until he dropped me back at my home. He was going to spend the afternoon looking at houses with his realtor and again there was no mention as to when we would see each other, because we both knew we would.

As soon as I got in the house, I grabbed my cigarettes and went into the backyard to smoke several in rapid succession. I started to allow myself to wonder what the problem was. Was it an injury of some sort? Was he impotent? Could I go on with a man who couldn't make love to me? And then all of a sudden, I realized there was no question about going on with him, to my great surprise. I was already in love with him.

The sun was about to set when Gary called me several days later. I took pride in the fact that I waited for him to call and still had not memorized his phone number. We spent a little while on the phone that evening. Gary told me about how he had a tendency to compartmentalize his life. I asked about his ex-wife. "Is there any chance that you would go back to her?"

There was a silent pause and then he said, "That's a scary thought." I took that as an answer and never mentioned her again. I realized that he was with me now, inescapably.

Gary wrapped his hand around the handle of the Thai restaurant's front door, opening it for me as I asked casually, "How old are you?"

"I'll be 59 in February. Scary."

"Don't say that! The last person who said that to me died that year. She was turning 47 and said she didn't like the sound of that number."

"Wow! Okay, I won't say that again."

After Gary perused the menu, he called the waiter over, asking, "Where are the stuffed chicken wings? I can't see them on the menu. You used to have them."

"These are new owners."

Gary closed the menu. "I wanted to introduce you to stuffed chicken wings. Do you want to stay here or go look for a place that has them?"

"Whatever you want."

We stayed and ordered. I unbuttoned the top of my jeans. Gary grinned, "She's about to eat!" He found my voracious appetite amusing. I could eat whatever and as much as I wanted without gaining weight. We enjoyed a lovely meal, after which he took me back to the condo and tenderly made love to me. He had told me at some point that he was jaded sexually, as he had had so much of it. He and his ex-wife had evidently engaged in almost every sort of sexual adventure—nudist camps, orgies, you name it.

He began by touching me with reverence, kissing me passionately until we were both burning. Our clothes fell to the floor. Laying me gently on his bed, he ducked down between my legs, kissing and sucking me with delight. I gave myself over to him entirely. Then he raised his magnificent body and perching gracefully above me, he entered me with all of his wonderful strength. Together we came in ecstasy. He held me in his arms wordlessly, as I laid my head upon his immense chest, all my fears gone away.

I had left Jessi with a babysitter at home. She was a fairly new massage therapist at work. She seemed intelligent and responsible, though I realize now I did not know her well enough to leave my child in her hands. She had offered to stay over at our house so Gary and I could spend the night together.

We rested in each other's arms until morning, then he took me home. He always picked me up and took me home. I never had to meet him anywhere; he was such a gentleman. We arrived back at my place to find that neither

Jessi nor the sitter were there. I began to panic immediately. I called her cell phone but there was no answer. I had only been to her home once. Gary insisted on driving me there.

"How could I have let her stay with my child?"

I was embarrassed for him to see me so hysterical, but he played the strong silent type, occasionally grasping my hand as he drove, rather than ridiculing me for panicking. He was gentle yet in control. His surety gave me confidence and helped me to calm down. When we pulled into her driveway I leapt out of the car, screaming. How could she be so irresponsible as to leave my house and not even leave a note or answer her cell phone? I never spoke to her again. Jessi hopped in the car, and Gary took us home.

I think it was on that drive that Jessi started to like him. He was cool and collected, like her. Gary and I had mutually decided to keep Jessi out of our relationship until we were sure we were going to stay together.

Gary came by on his way out of work a few evenings later for the massage I had encouraged him to take. He was working out of two offices, each only a few miles down the road from us in opposite directions. At one he did referrals for high-profile clients, mostly needing rehab centers. He'd counsel them until he could persuade them to get help, then send them to the center most appropriate for them—Cottonwood, Hazelton. At the other office was his private practice.

Jessi greeted him warmly for the first time when he arrived that night. I led him into my beautiful office, with its large louvered windows, lace drapes, and a full wall bookcase in dark wood. My massage table was state of the art in serious black. I instructed him as I did everyone. "Take everything off. You can leave your underwear on, if you wish, and lay face down on the table between the sheets. I'll be back in a moment." Then I left, closing the door behind me.

When I returned, I began as I always did, my hands held open an inch or two above his upper back, as I silently prayed the short prayer that I said over everyone before beginning the massage and whenever I paused to use Chi Gung. It was a way of centering myself as I waited to feel the heat from the client's body. When the energy connected, I began.

I remember he moaned softly when he first felt the touch of my palm on him. The moaning ended there, as I found continuous moaning throughout a massage extremely obnoxious. He was impressed with my ability, but I wasn't fully cognizant of the fact that he was no stranger to me. We were already very close, and that closeness might cause me to overlook something, like the fact that his hands swelled during the massage. I had never seen that in any of the thousands of patients I had treated, yet I passed it off as unusual, though unimportant.

It was toward the end of the massage when he turned over that I suddenly saw an American Native Chief laying on the table. I looked away and saw Jessi and I dressed in authentic native garb, walking down a dirt road to keep the chief company. It wasn't unusual for me to have clients transform on the table, though never quite like this. And the added vision of Jessi and I was completely out of the ordinary. What did it mean? I wondered. Afterwards he left, as I had asked him to, but not before he expressed his heartfelt gratitude. "That was the best massage I ever had."

I didn't tell him about the chief at that time. I did, however, share the story with Jessi. It was she who would tell him sometime later.

All the Hanukkah lights had burned away, and the Christmas season was soon upon us. Jessi and I celebrated both. It had started when we were living with my mother. Mother had not been raised as a Jew, though she was by blood. She had celebrated Christmas all her life, as did my brother Joseph. So I set up the artificial Christmas tree my father bought years before, and Jessi had her first Christmas the year she was born. I taught her nothing of Christianity, as I wanted her to find her own way. There are times when I think that Christ deserved better from me but at the same time, I did not want her to suffer, as I had, at the foot of a Cross.

I felt deeply bound to my Jewish core. In my anxiety about assimilation I tried to make Hanukkah bigger than Christmas. Jessi received one gift on the first day, two gifts on the second, and so on. Ridiculous, I know presents have nothing to do with the true meaning and remembrance of Hanukkah. Judaism is a culture of tradition and the religion of law, so we celebrated all the Jewish holidays.

I taught Jessi how to light the candles for Shabbat, because as a Jew I felt she needed to know this. There was no religious intent on my part. Despite the fact that I had lived as an Orthodox Jew in Israel and for some time in America as well, I found such austerity brought forth a kind of arrogance in me that was self-defeating in relation to my personal goals. I attended the temple within myself, cherishing the love I found there. Gary said, "What I like about being a Jew is that I can practice the holidays I want to practice, not practice the holidays I don't want to practice, and I'm still a Jew!"

My mother came to stay with us over the Christmas holidays as always. Gary told me he was going up north to his sister's because his niece was having some surgery related to breast cancer and he wanted to be there to support her and his sister. He would be gone until just after New Year's and asked if he could take me out to dinner before he left, the day after Christmas.

As usual, I was always practically panting up till the moment he arrived and then a deep calm came over me as I opened the door to greet him. I introduced him to my mother. Jessi was still shy in the background. Gary took me to a pricey Italian restaurant known for good food and service. We sat by the bay window overlooking the lake. I remember his beautiful face across from me. I asked for bread, and the waiter brought it cold and dry, obviously left over from the day before. Gary could see by my expression that I was dissatisfied.

I explained, "It's cold and old."

He called the waiter back and asked him to bring us some fresh hot bread. The guy took it, heated the same bread, and brought it back to us! I wish I could say that my entrée went better, but unfortunately, no. I ordered shrimp over pasta for what I now realize was the very last time in my life. I am often tempted but have never been willing to try that again. Shrimp must be completely fresh to be flavorful. Once it sours, it's inedible.

I remember these little things, but there we were together, and I could feel him loving me and me loving him. The way we were drawn to each other was powerful and secure, yet gentle like the satisfaction of feet touching ground.

He made it all up to me in the parking lot that night. Gary really gave himself to the kissing. The passion, the burning, and the flames were amazing, and we literally created steam against the windows. We drew back for a breath. I touched his gorgeous biceps with my fingertips.

"I was never attracted to anyone built like you before, too intimidating. But now, my gentle giant, this is what I want."

I didn't elaborate on what "this" was. It was his strength I needed. Gary went three times a week to the gym early in the morning, working out with weights. He was the picture of perfect health and longevity. He leaned over to kiss me once more, then took me home.

It was long after I had stopped asking the question or even wondering why Gary and his wife had divorced, when Shane called to tell me. "Listen, I know you've been wondering about Gary's divorce. Well, I've been waiting for him to tell you but I think you should know. She left him for a woman. They were involved in a three-way relationship for a year or so when suddenly she left Gary, running off with the other woman. Six months later she came and begged him to take her back, but he refused."

"Wow. Thanks for telling me."

"I just thought you should know."

I hung up the phone and let it sink in. I didn't care about anything. Just that we were together now and I could feel him in my bones.

We saw each other immediately upon his return. He was anxious to see me, so he picked me up from work. As we drove through the daylight, Gary told me about his adventures up north. His niece had made it through the surgery well, and his sister was grateful for him being there. He said on the last day he had come upon an interesting shop, then added with some reservation, as if the thought itself confused him, "I wanted to buy you a ring, but I bought you a rock instead!" It was a very heavy beautiful blue rock with a hole carved in it to place a tea candle. It still sits on my desk.

Gary's birthday was approaching. "I want to spend my birthday exactly the way I want to," he said, almost as if I would object, which seemed like something he carried from the past.

"And what exactly would you like to do?" I was almost holding my breath. What would he say? What did he want?

"I want to eat Thai food on my bed with you and watch *The Sheltering Sky*. It was a 2 hour-20-minute movie by Bertolucci, starring John Malkovich and Debra Winger. Highly existentialist, it revolves around three Americans traveling together on a seemingly aimless wandering journey that starts in Tangiers and takes them deep into the Sahara Desert, winding through a relationship trilogy beneath the sheltering sky. Why this movie in particular? It was his favorite. Only at this moment, do I understand why.

We picked up the Thai food and headed back to the condo. I had picked lovely, almost sheer, patterned harem pants and a skintight black top to wear for him as we sat on his bed that night. We carefully laid out the multi-plated Thai feast on the duvet before us. When I handed Gary his gift, he nearly leapt off the bed with delight. It was a copy of *The Inner Game of Golf* by W. Timothy Gallwey. I had managed to get it signed by the author himself because his secretary was one of my clients. Gary and I made love long before the movie ended, until we both slept like angels in each other's arms.

That night I had an extremely complicated dream that I have not forgotten. In the dream Gary introduced me to his entire family. I was wearing my beautiful black velvet pumps that I saved to wear only on the most special occasions. There was a baseball diamond symbolizing the part of my family I feel most distanced from. His family treated me rather rudely, for the most part, except the stepson, who treated me with some kindness. There was a campus with many young people wandering about, and a flock of birds flew wildly through the air. At the end of the dream I looked down and noticed that my beautiful black velvet shoes were covered with mud.

I told Gary about the dream on the way home that morning. He asked me what I thought it meant. I told him I didn't know but that I thought it was trying to tell me something. We both felt the muddied shoes were significant but had no idea of what.

It wasn't long afterwards, on our way out to dinner, he took me on a side trip as the sun blazed before setting. "I want to show you something. It's a house I'm thinking about buying. My agent just showed it to me this morning."

"Okay."

He had not taken me on any of his previous house searches but now he had found one he wanted me to see. I was intrigued but I dared not dream that it meant what it could mean, that he wanted to see if I liked the house, maybe to buy it for us.

We arrived in the cul-de-sac of Kiva Court, where this beautiful home was. There were two giant ancient oak trees standing majestically in front, just to the side. Around them were large boulders, wide and flat enough to sit on, in an area cleared almost as if a meeting could happen there.

He parked in the driveway, and though he didn't have the keys, we walked around peering through the windows. The sunken living room had a 20 ft. vaulted ceiling with a full front window facing the oaks. We went around the back to the pool, looking into the den and kitchen by the French doors, as the sun lit the last shadows of the day.

"I love it!" I blurted out. I just couldn't help myself. It was truly so lovely, all of it. Nothing more was said as we drove away. The next day he called me.

"I bought the house! I couldn't wait to tell you!"

I hardly knew how to respond. Did he do it for us? No one had ever done such a thing for me. Could it be?

"Wow! That's wonderful. Congratulations!"

"Yeah, I have the keys, we can go in now. I'll show you tomorrow, if you have time."

"I'll make time!"

Meanwhile, Jessi's fifth grade class was going on a natural science camping retreat. It would mean two nights away and I was having difficulty signing the permission slip. Gary was so sweet and kind about it. He convinced me to let her go. I trusted his instinct and felt confident enough to take his advice. It was a very big deal to me because I had never allowed her to be that far away from me for that long. Naturally, Gary won a lot of points with Jessi for that influence. I think she began to see that he might be a good way to balance me. She was always far more understanding than I even expected she could be.

With the camping trip on, Gary would have a chance to lay with me for the very first time in my own bed. It was exciting. He took me to dinner locally. Then we went back to my place. It was a night of extraordinary, explosive passion. We burned together. I was on top bracing myself, gripping his magnificent arms so tightly there would be deep bruises in his biceps. He left early for his morning workout and called me later to say that the guys at the gym were remarking about his bruises.

"Oh, sorry!"

"It's okay! I like it."

I stepped out back to have a smoke and noticed the porch light had exploded in its socket. I was immediately concerned that I might be pregnant, surmising that the light bulb had exploded when we did. It was possibly a powerful entry. I knew the way we women always know.

Gary had told me so many times that he did not want to have his own children. I discussed his reluctance with one of my wonderful patients who was a forensic psychologist. I'd given her some history, specifically that when he was 18 his older sister had given birth to a child with Down's syndrome, who soon died. I asked her if she thought that could possibly have anything to do with his reluctance. She explained to me that yes, young men around that age are often extremely sensitive, and that it was quite possible it made such a deep impression on him, he didn't want to risk making children of his own.

I did wish I could bring Jessi a sibling, but he seemed so fiercely against it I did not want to risk our relationship. I did not even wait a day. I was so concerned that I might be pregnant I went and got the morning-after pill. In the kit they give you a test so you can see if you are actually pregnant. I did not take the test. I just took the pills. It would only be a few weeks later, when we were sitting together on the sofa in the den of our new home, that he would look at me and say, quite out of the blue, "I may be changing my mind about having children."

Gary had shown increasing interest in learning more about what my Teacher had to offer. He was with me often now after my practicing, as we were together frequently. I would go to the other room early in the morning to practice. He noticed the peaceful reset that occurred in me, so eventually we went together to see a public video presentation of my Teacher.

I walked with him up to the front row, where I always like to sit. The event lasted only 45 minutes. As soon as we stood up to leave, Gary rushed ahead of me in long strides down the aisle. He saw someone he knew, an old friend of mine, and apparently his. It was Giancarlo, the UCLA physics professor turned master marble worker. It was he who had spoken the night my parents came with me so many years ago. There they were, Gary and Giancarlo, locked in a bear hug, overjoyed to see each other again. I was a bit stunned, and they were both amused by the surprised look on my face.

Giancarlo explained in his slight Italian accent, "We know each other."

"I hope so!" I remarked with a grin.

Nothing further was said until we reached the car, when Gary told me, "He came to see me a few times, some years ago."

I couldn't resist asking him, "Any impressions about my Teacher?"

"I'd like to hear more."

I told him I would get him a video that he could watch at home. Nothing else was said.

The bar mitzvah of Patty and Eli's youngest son was coming up. Everyone in the Israeli community I had known for so many years would be there. I sat with them at the family table, as I had at their first son's bar mitzvah. I had helped both of her boys write their speeches. Their first son was beloved to me, and unexpectedly added an addendum to his speech, thanking me for having been the strongest influence in his life. Five hundred jaws dropped open, including mine.

I wanted to attend with Gary. It would be the only time I had anybody with me in all these years since Zohar's death. Gary wasn't very enthusiastic about it, however. For him it would be just another bar mitzvah he felt obliged to attend. But that decision would never need to be made, because Patty and Eli refused to allow me to bring him, saying, "We don't know him."

"I know him. That's not good enough for you?"

"Ah no, actually it's not. Eli would go crazy if you brought some stranger."

"Really? Half your attendees are mafia kingpins and my nationally renowned psychologist lover is not good enough for you?"

I should never have attended under those circumstances, but for the sake of their child, I did. Gary made plans to move into the house that weekend. His sister from up north was coming down to help him. I offered to help as well, but he wanted to do it on his own.

Jessi and I were to meet them at their house and go in the limo from there. Patty was rushing around half hysterical when I arrived. She was delegating and ordering me around but I know what it's like to be in that state of mind, so I gave her some leeway. She gave me a bag of grass with some papers, told me go in the bathroom, roll some joints, and stuff them in her purse, which I did. I myself would not have dared to bring pot to a bar mitzvah, especially not theirs. Next she told me to go upstairs and get an empty pillowcase for the money that would be given in the tens of thousands. Then into the limo and off we went.

The Olympic Collection was a palatial banquet center for the ultra-rich to hold their weddings, bar mitzvahs, and bat mitzvahs. There would be 500 people attending as there was at Edon's bar mitzvah a few years before. I felt, as usual, as if I was the only single person there, the only one without a mate present, outside of a few widows and a smattering of bachelors on the hunt for young blood. Divorced or widowed, it seemed no one stayed unmarried for long in this community.

The fact that I was 45 and had never been married was fodder to be whispered over. I suppose it meant to them that there must be something seriously wrong with me. I could never have married for money, position, or fame. Now at last I was in love again, and I was surer every day that Gary loved me. I missed him being there with me and I did feel lonely.

Patty told me that I was to light the last candle but somewhere in the night her attitude changed towards me. I could not have imagined why and would not be told until the next day, when Patty accused me of stealing the joints out of her purse. Jessi told me later that the kids were smoking something on the side of the building, but she didn't know what. I figured out who took it later but never told Patty or confronted the person responsible. I let it go. It wasn't the worst that evening had to offer me.

I stood waiting in the background as the candle-lighting ceremony went forward, all 15 candles, until the time came for the last one. Patty and Eli were up in front of everyone and Eli said, "I can't read this. I am sorry. It seems someone tore the last name off."

Patty leaned over and whispered into Eli's ear. He gave her a strange look, shrugged his shoulders, and they lit the last one together.

Then Eli took back the microphone and said, "Thank you everyone and a special thanks to Jessi's mom, wherever she is."

He placed his hand above his eyes as if he was peering through the crowd trying to see where I was. I was there, completely mortified, everyone staring at me. I finally understood that "thank you" from Eli was 23 years and one minute too late. Instead of honoring our friendship, I was publicly humiliated.

I went outside and privately broke down for a few moments. When I was finally able to gain control of myself, I called Gary. I pretended to be cool when all I wanted was to hear his voice and feel the love within it. I asked him how the move had gone. He said they were done but very tired. He wanted to pick me up the next day and go shopping for the house.

As for Patty and Eli, I was done with them. When she called me the next day to accuse me of taking the joints from her purse, I told her that if after all these years she could imagine that I would do that to her, let alone at her son's bar mitzvah, I did not want her as a friend anymore.

Gary put down the ragtop of his Mustang, and we headed out on Ventura Boulevard. He told me that when he lived with his ex-wife, everything in the house had been her pick, and this time he wanted the choices to be his. The first stop was at Bed Bath and Beyond for towels. Together we chose sets in jewel tones of yellow, emerald, and burgundy.

As we lifted the towels into the cart, I casually told him, "I bought a beautiful black bikini for the summer."

"Why does it make me reel when you say that?"

Did he not think we would still be together by summer? No, that was not it. It was something else. Something neither of us expected, that I would understand all too soon.

The house was taking shape though there was not a stick of furniture in the living room and we were looking for a Parsons table to put in the dining room. His desk was already in the upstairs office, though several boxes of files were still on the floor in the foyer.

As he hadn't been to a doctor in many years, I was naturally concerned about his health and asked him to see the famous local diagnostician, Dr. Edd. Gary agreed that it might be time to check in and promised to go.

"I'll do it once these boxes are upstairs."

The master bedroom was very large and included a landing with a seating area. Gary's antique Chinese headboard with a black lacquered background and colorful figurines painted on it, the matching night stands, and the huge carved armoire fit perfectly and looked absolutely beautiful.

Soon enough, although Jessi and I had not moved in yet, we were staying over from time to time.

One morning, as Gary and I wandered around the bedroom with our sleepy yawns and stretches, Gary said, "I want to change the carpet in here to a different color."

"Forest green would be nice."

"I'll decide," he said with a trace of resentment left over from life with his ex, then he added, "I was thinking maybe forest green."

I was quiet for a few moments, "You know for the first three months of our relationship I referred to you as 'what's-his-name'." A broad smile came across Gary's face. This was the full extent of our arguing, a little rub followed by a snarky retort.

I smiled and excused myself saying I'd see him in an hour. I grabbed two pillows off our bed and took them with me into the still empty room next to our bedroom. This will be Jessi's room, I thought. I closed the door behind me and went into the closet to shut out the exterior light. I arranged the pillows comfortably and sat down to practice. How beautiful the feeling within inside of me! How wonderful to be alive and in love! I gave my attention to the comfort within me and filled myself with its resounding peace.

When I rejoined Gary in the kitchen, my bristling energy was bouncing with bliss. There was a bright smile on my face. I hoisted myself up on the edge of the kitchen counter and did the peacock pose, perfectly level with the floor. I held it for a moment, then stood back on my feet. I enjoyed being free, and he enjoyed watching me. Gary smiled broadly, drew me close to him, held me against his chest, looked deep into my eyes, and I into his. No kiss, just the look of love. There were no words, no validations, only love itself, manifesting its presence between us. This was it. We were set.

Shane, the beautiful young woman who had introduced Gary and me, came by again for a massage. She asked how Gary and I were doing. I told her how happy we were, so very much in love though neither one of us had stated it. "I'm still a little scared, I suppose. At the same time, it feels as if we'll be together for the rest of our lives."

Shane was lying face down on the table as I worked on her, when all of a sudden she said, "I don't know if Gary can do it. It's something about his heart."

I leapt, without questioning, to an easy conclusion. "Yes, I know his heart was badly broken in the past."

Then another unreferenced thought popped out of her mouth, "There's something about a dog." She described the dog, but I knew nothing of him. So I thought perhaps she was talking about a dog we'd buy together. Another warning I missed entirely.

Gary told me he was thinking about driving back up north on Mother's Day weekend to visit his sister again. I had the strongest feeling that he wanted to invite me but was concerned about taking me from Jessi.

One day when it was pouring rain, I left work early and on my way home I thought about Gary. I thought, Maybe just drive a little further. Go see him. Surprise him for lunch. But I did not. I talked myself out of it and when I later told him, he said he would have been really happy to see me.

"Great, then I will sometime!"

We agreed it was time to bring Jessi into our relationship. We were ready. He picked us up together early Saturday afternoon and took us home to his place. Among the file boxes still in the foyer were Native American artifacts, protected in plexiglass boxes. Jessi noticed them as soon as we came in. It must have reminded her of the story I had told her about the chief, because in a moment alone with Gary, she told him. A little while later that same day I thought to tell him the story myself but as I began, he quickly stopped me, smiling, and said, "Jessi just told me that one."

I was surprised and pleased.

Jessi took a swim in the pool while Gary and I started preparing dinner together. He was marinating meat for our barbecue, and I was making my mother's wonderful potato salad. He casually told me he was showing the house to his ex and two stepchildren the following day.

"I guess I just want to show off the new place to let the kids know I'm okay."

The kids, his stepchildren, a boy and a girl, were now in their 30s. The son was still a bachelor, and the daughter was married with three children. She, like her mother, was also a psychologist turned attorney. After having her first child she decided she just couldn't bear to go through pregnancy again, so she hired a surrogate who gave birth to twins. Gary referred to them as Romulus and Remus because by the age of four they were quite the giants. He passed off the ex coming as no big deal. I offered and made enough potato salad for both occasions.

When Jessi was dried off and dressed, she joined us in the kitchen. All of a sudden, she started crawling around on the floor like a crocodile.

"What are you doing?" I asked her.

"Don't worry, she's just enjoying being free." Gary said without the slightest sign of anything but delight. Adding to the drama, I cut my fingers badly twice in a row while chopping onions. After the second chop I declared while he bandaged me, "I want you to know, I am not a cutter!"

"Just be careful," he added, "we don't want to spend the night in the Emergency Room."

Jessi slept on the sofa in the den that night because we didn't have a bed in her room yet. I remember Gary's neck had really been hurting him. I massaged it a couple of times, iced it, and attempted to heal it with Chi Gung. He had been terribly ill just the week before, so ill that he called to say he could not come to get me, breaking our date for the first and only time. I wanted to go to him, and I knew he wouldn't stop me, but there was a fierce wind out that night and I was afraid to drive. So I trusted his assertion that he would be all right and did not go to him, though I felt quite ill at ease about it.

Only a few days before that incident, we had been sitting together in a pizza shop waiting for baked ziti to go, when Gary seemed unusually tired, almost weak.

"Are you okay?"

"Yeah, I'm just tired. I was so tired earlier today I asked the housekeeper to go home and come back tomorrow."

He put his hand on my knee. "I'll be okay."

I could tell his neck was still bothering him though he made love to me that night until I was muffling my screams. I pulled him back up next to me and laid my head on his great and wonderful chest, falling asleep in his arms.

In the morning I stayed beside him as he told me the story of his beloved dog who had been hit by a car and died several days later. It was obvious that he still missed him as his eyes welled up with tears. Just then Jessi burst into the room and jumped in bed with us.

"What was all that noise last night?" she asked, slyly. "The ceiling was shaking, I thought maybe it was an earthquake."

"Not an earthquake, but next time you'll sleep upstairs here with us. I'll have a bed ready for you in the other room." Gary replied.

Jessi seemed content. She laid her head next to mine on his chest, so large we would need a dog to fill it.

I had prepared jachnun from scratch and brought it with me to cook overnight in the oven. We woke to the fragrance of fresh bread baking. Each of us dished up our own plates with the jachnun, homemade tahini, and freshly grated tomatoes, highly spiced. Then we sat outside all together to eat on the large bench-like rocks beneath the giant twin oaks. Afterwards, Gary invited us to take a short walk up the greenbelt with him before heading back.

Later that Sunday morning when he took us home, for the first time ever he did not pull into the driveway. I felt there was something strange about it. We both hopped out of the car, thanking him, waving goodbye, and saying cheerfully, "See you soon!" We had arranged to meet again on the Wednesday.

On Tuesday, April 20th 1999, I returned home from work in the afternoon, unaware of the terrible massacre that had taken place at Columbine. The phone rang. It was Gary's older sister Sharon.

"Are you Gary's friend?"

"Gary Allen?"

"Yes, I'm his sister."

"Oh, hello. How nice to hear from you. Are you the sister from up north? I was hoping to meet you soon."

"Yes, I'm Sharon.

"He loves you so much!"

"I've been searching for your number since early this morning."

"What's going on? He's all right, isn't he?"

"No, I am very sorry to tell you, Gary is dead. He died at three this morning of heart failure."

"No, that cannot be true. We are supposed to see each other tomorrow!"

"I am so sorry. He's gone. We wouldn't have even known to look for you, but he called your name throughout the night." There was true compassion in her voice. She tried to be as gentle as she could. Her patience with me was a testament to her kindness.

"What happened to him?"

"He went into his office at the referral center yesterday morning and collapsed. He had been drinking, possibly up all night, and when he went into his office, he must have blacked out. He hit his head against the desk on his way down, which gave him a concussion as well. He was drowning in his own vomit when they found him on the floor. His organs were already starting to shut down by the time the ambulance got him to the hospital. They think he might have had a small heart attack in the office, then another heart attack late in the afternoon. He never fully regained consciousness, though he struggled until the end to survive. Your name was the last word he spoke."

By now I was pacing around the backyard in horrified disbelief, struggling not to let everything inside of me collapse like a house of cards. Jessi came running to me from her bedroom. She could feel what was happening to me, tugging at my clothes.

"Mom, what is it?"

"No! He cannot be dead!"

"Mom! Who are you talking to!"

"It's Gary's sister."

"Mom, what's happened?"

Jessi placed both of her hands gently upon me. I asked Sharon to hang on a minute. By now I was all but collapsing against the sidewall of the house. Somehow, I held it together another few moments. Just then the mother of Jessi's schoolmate walked in the front door, through the house, and out to the backyard to find me. I grabbed her, whispered in her ear what was happening, and asked her to take Jessi with her.

"It's okay honey, just go with them. I'll explain later."

Jessi left reluctantly. I screamed furiously into the phone. "No, you don't understand. This just happened to me 12 years ago. I lost my beloved in Israel. This cannot be happening again! He cannot be dead!"

I can imagine now how helpless Sharon must've felt at that moment wondering if there was anything she could do for me. As if she could change the news. As if she too wasn't in agony. She just kept saying, "I am so sorry."

It took 45 minutes for her to convince me that he was dead. There were several moments of painful silence followed by, "I'm really sorry to ask you this now, but the family has a few questions for you." She waited another minute. "How long have you and Gary known each other?"

"What difference does that make?"

"We were just wondering."

"Long enough to be deeply in love."

"Did Gary ever speak to you about whether he wanted to be buried or cremated?"

"Oh, God," I said, barely audibly. "Cremated."

"And what about his eyes?"

"Don't touch his eyes!" I blurted out, then, "I am sorry, I don't know. He never spoke of it."

"Okay."

"Listen," I said, "may I get your phone number and call you back if I need to. I need to be alone now."

"Of course."

She gave me her number and I hung up the phone. Now standing by myself in the kitchen I felt as if the walls were closing in on me. I wanted to run away but there was no place to run to that would free me from this. I called my dear friend Ronnie. I had never known her to answer the phone on the first ring before, and it would be the shortest conversation of our lives. As soon as I heard her say hello, I told her, "Gary's dead."

"Oh my God."

I could feel her quaking for me over the phone. She was well aware of what I went through when Zohar died.

"How do you feel?"

"I feel like running away, but there is nowhere to run to."

"What do you want to do?"

"I want to go inside but I am afraid."

"What are you afraid of?"

"I am afraid I'll find Gary there."

"Well, if you go to where love is you will find love; you know you don't need to be afraid of love."

"Okay, I'll do it!"

I hung up the phone, went into my room and sat down to practice. But before beginning I decided to call Dr. Edd. I wanted to ask a doctor who had nothing to do with the case how it was that Gary died and did that mean I was about to die. Dr. Edd was kind enough to get on the phone with me for a few moments. "Yes, you are going to die. We're all going to die but you're not going to die of what he did just now."

"How could he have just died like that? There was nothing wrong with him! At least he didn't think there was anything wrong with him. His neck was hurting him, but beyond that, nothing wrong with him."

"There was something wrong with him, and in all likelihood, he knew it!"

I released the phone and surrendered to practice. How incredible that traces of peace could still be felt within me. The love began again to bubble up from within, floating off the surface of my heart. That's when I felt him. It was as if Gary was standing in the room right next to me.

"Oh my God." I leapt up immediately. "He can see that my room is a mess," I thought, grabbing a cigarette. "And now he's going to know that I smoke. Oh well, too late now." I lit up, took the phone, and dialed Sharon back.

"Where is he? Where is Gary's body?"

She was a little frantic. "I don't know. I'm not sure. Still at the hospital I would think."

"What hospital?"

"Encino."

"Thanks."

I called the hospital and in short order had the right person on the phone. Once I'd determined that Gary's body was still there, I gave my orders, "Don't touch him! Don't let anyone touch him! I'm coming right now. I will be there in 15 minutes!"

"Okay. It's okay. We won't touch him. He is still here."

Jessi got back before I left. I sat down on the sofa with her, still crying. "Gary's dead, honey, I'm so sorry."

"I know Mommy. She told me."

"I need to go see him."

She grasped my hand. "I am coming with you."

I told Jessi to wait outside while I entered the small room. I wanted to spare her any more pain, unaware that she could see my face through the windowed door. There were two steel refrigerated drawers in the wall. The orderly pulled out the bottom drawer and then left me alone with him. There laid Gary, my sweet gentle giant, not yet cold as a stone. I kissed his chest and laid my head upon it for the last time. I drew back the eyelids of his dark brown eyes; they were still there, as if able to see me. I closed them and told him, "I love you with all my heart." Then I kissed his lips and pushed the drawer back shut.

Beyond that, I recall very little about what transpired between Jessi and I or anything else in those first blind hours. I just remember pacing around on the wooden floors of the living room, asking God over and over again, "Why did you do this? Why did you take him from me like this?"

Every time I asked, I would see the same vision in my head. It was of Gary's car flipping over on the road. Suddenly I understood that God was going to take him anyway. He took him now, like this, so that Gary did not take me with him. I remembered that Gary was concerned about inviting me to join him on the trip up north, not wanting to take me away from Jessi.

The next morning, upon waking, I had a clear vision that Gary was standing by the barbecue where he had just cooked for us at the new house only days before. He was waiting for us to come. It was so clear I did not need a second thought. I told Jessi, "We need to go to the house right now. Gary's waiting for us." She did not ask me how a dead man could be waiting for us. She just came along. What a dear one she is, my sweet angel, my dear friend.

When we arrived at the house, the front door was wide open. Who do you suppose I would find standing in his kitchen, fumbling through his things, but his ex-wife and her son, Gary's beloved stepson. The stepson asked if he could speak with me outside for a moment. He walked me over to where the twin oaks stood and asked me what I knew about Gary's cocaine use.

"Excuse me?" I said.

"I take it you didn't know?"

"What are you talking about?"

"We found a bag of cocaine in Gary's pocket at the hospital when we were looking for the keys. We came here to try to get it if there's anymore. I mean we wouldn't want anyone to find it!"

"I don't even understand what you're saying?"

He finally realized that I was entirely dumbfounded and didn't have a clue what he was talking about. And that it was clearly a shock to me Gary did cocaine at all. It turns out that Gary had been drinking heavily and continuing to do coke until the morning. Did he have to get totally loaded just to see his ex? The young man assured me as we walked back up to the house that they hadn't found anything more.

Moments later he walked Jessi out back by the poolside to quiz her. I don't remember what few things the ex might have asked me. I did not actually see her, though I was looking straight at her. I only remember that at a certain moment I was feeling quite weak, so I just looked at her and said, "I'm going to have to go lie down."

She got it, that it was time for her to leave, that she did not belong here. She needed to go. The young man reappeared with Jessi, who wrapped her arms around my waist and gently hugged me. Then, thank God, they left and I closed the door behind them.

I crawled onto our unmade bed and fell like a crumpled rag on the rustled sheets. I felt like half my body had been ripped off my bones. There was no way to stop the aching and the emptiness. I had exhausted myself lamenting and was quite likely dehydrated from weeping. I grasped the sheets around me and smelled them. I held his pillow to my face and inhaled deeply his lingering fragrance. I felt the warmth of his presence all around me as the smell filled my memory. Jessi came to get me off the bed, leading me downstairs and outside to the pool.

"Come Mother," she said, patting the space beside her. "Sit down here and put your feet into the water."

I obeyed her like a child. She sat very close to me. Some years later I would overhear her saying, "I tried to help her through it when Gary died."

It was true. Aside from the fact that I could not allow myself to collapse because of her, she was dependent upon me to stay sane. It was also true and much more so, that it was by her efforts and her kindness I survived. She would try to distract me a little here and there. She would burst out singing, "Baby Love" from the Supremes, then I'd join in and the next thing we knew, we were happy for a moment.

The lawyer's wife, Shane's mother, came to the door with large sandwiches, coleslaw, and chips from the deli. It was good. Jessi needed to eat, though I was not at all hungry. Perhaps that's why it is a law in Judaism that one must continue to eat though the beloved has died, first of all because it revives life and because it forestalls the danger of starving oneself. I hungered only for him. I wandered around as if in a daze and yet I could feel him near me as if he was standing right next to me sometimes. I raised my arms up and felt his huge embrace.

Opening the fridge, I saw a whole platter of perfectly carved lamb, which seemed intended for us this very day. There was also a partially-eaten loaf of brie that had been split and filled with sun-dried tomatoes, roasted pine nuts, and fresh basil leaves. When I was finally able to take a taste, it was wonderful.

I woke early the next morning. Jessi was still sleeping sweetly beside me. I got up, went to the comfortable chair in the annex of the bedroom, and sat down, drawing a sheet over me. I let myself surrender to the love that washed up within me. It brought new meaning to the phrase, "You are sitting on your flotation cushion."

I wandered into the upstairs office he'd barely begun to put together. I sat at his desk and opened the main drawer. There was the key attached to the realtor's card, the key for me. Next to it was a ring box. I opened it. There was a beautiful ring in it. I put it on my finger. I could feel it was his though I had never seen him wear it. I went outside by the twin oaks and sat on the rock bench where we had sat together eating jachnun. Suddenly I saw him as clearly as the trees before me, standing straight and tall. I ran to him, throwing my arms around his precious energy. He told me he loved me and that he was sorry to go, and I told him that I love him too. I was wearing the ring. He picked up my hand kissed it, saying of the ring, "I want you to keep this. It's for you." I lingered with him a long while until I had to let go, to let him go.

Jessi and I sat shiva in Gary's home for all seven days. In the beginning few days his presence was most profound.

One evening it was as if he had put a note on the kitchen table saying, "I'm going to my sister's. I'll be back soon." And he did come back. He seemed to spend most of the time there with us, watching over us, and seeing me tear myself apart. Why did I not know something was so terribly wrong with him?

I tracked down the coroner who was about to do the autopsy. I spoke with him just before he opened the drawer where Gary's body now lay. I demanded of him, "I want you to crack open his chest and tell me why he died! Don't just run a panel. I need to know why he died." I was having difficulty choking back my tears.

The very kind doctor said, "Okay, I'll call you back as soon as I'm done. It'll be about 45 minutes." I waited with bated breath. He did call back on time.

"Did Gary know he had heart disease?"

"Heart disease?"

"Well, his cholesterol was over 600. Also, he had a rare condition known as a dissecting aortic aneurysm. It is very difficult to detect, and when it split, he would've bled to death in a minute and a half."

"So there was nothing to be done even if we had detected the heart disease earlier?"

"Possibly, but the dissecting aneurysm would have made his survival from the necessary surgery unlikely."

Gary's private patients continued to call the house for a while looking for him, and I would have to tell them he was dead.

One woman said to me, "Are you her?"

"Her?"

"Gary's woman."

"Yes."

"My husband and I were having couples' therapy with Gary. He told us he had finally found the relationship with you that he sought all of his life."

"Thank you so much for telling me."

There were some thoughts spoken around family and friends that Gary, as he was going anyway, wanted to get to heaven on time to help the kids arriving from the Columbine massacre. It would be just like him as he was also a grief therapist. Everyone wanted to give meaning or a reason for the unimaginable that is death. Now the dream I had that morning made sense.

His family arranged for his memorial to be held in a beautiful temple. It was designed in the shape of a hexagram, like the Star of David. There was an uncomfortable flurry among the family members, who were for the most part polite, though unwelcoming. Jessi and I were seated stage right from the pulpit. His ex and her grown children were sitting directly across the room from us. Outside of the family, only the patients in whom Gary had confided in could even guess who I was.

I was not invited to speak. Oh, if I really felt compelled to, there is nothing that could've stopped me. In my grief it had not occurred to me that I would even want to, and though for a moment I thought of it, I was too weak to stand. It was all I could do to contain my disbelief. The lawyer came up to me and made some remark about the interesting positioning of the old wife and the new. Yeah, I got it. The lawyer's family sat directly behind us.

His wife leaned over and whispered in my ear, "I've seen Gary."

"What?"

"Gary is here."

"I know."

"He told me it's beautiful to be so free that he can pass through walls."

I was happy to know that I wasn't the only one who could see him.

Afterwards there was a gathering at his younger sister's house in Encino, to which Jessi and I were also invited. His 92-year-old mother was sitting alone at the kitchen snack bar. I made a point of going to sit next to her and introduced myself.

"Oh yes, I heard about you."

Then her thoughts seemed to wander off.

"I should have helped him," she said. "I should've stood up to his father."

Suddenly I knew what she was talking about. Gary had vaguely mentioned that there had been an incident between his father and him while they were playing together in the garage one day. He had never explained what happened, he stopped short and became silent.

Gary did tell me about a 45-year-old Persian patient of his, who had a wife and two young children. The wife knew every time he bought a pack of cigarettes on Friday that he would be checking into a hotel for the weekend to do cocaine. This behavior had only begun recently when the man was at the top of his game. With Gary, all had been accomplished and seemingly he should have been comfortable and happy with himself. Instead, the memory of childhood sexual abuse haunted him.

I could hardly wait to get out of there and go back to the house where I could feel close to Gary. I gave my sincere condolences to his mother and every other member of the family. We were only there a little while when that same

Persian couple showed up at the front door. They said they had been at the memorial but had not had a chance to express their condolences to us before we left, and so they took a chance that we would be here and stopped by. She was a beautiful zaftig woman still wearing the pale-yellow hat that she had worn in the temple earlier. And he was, exactly as I recall Gary had once commented, a very handsome man. I invited them in for a moment. They were considerate enough not to stay very long. Then Jessi and I walked out the door.

Jessi and I were still living hand to mouth. Gary and I had never spoken about finances, and I'm sure he had no idea how tight things were for us despite the fact that I drove a ten-year-old car, with paint peeling off the roof, hood, and trunk. Gary had told me there was a couple hundred dollars in change in the house. It was actually not quite that much. We had to use it to survive in these seven days that I was not able to work.

My mother even sent me a little money to help us hang on. When his family discovered the missing change, they behaved as if I had stolen something from him. They ended up taking the house, the car, all of his possessions including a $100,000 life insurance policy that he had just purchased but had not yet written the name of the beneficiary, leaving me only with his body, which I would not have traded for anything in the world. It was my duty to take care of him, as when the body of Mark Antony was delivered to Cleopatra. She anointed him and prepared him for burial, as I would now do for my beloved.

All that was left was to wait for his body to be released from the coroner's office. The family had left it to me to pick the crematorium where his remains would be delivered. I interviewed several places and chose the one where the man who ran it struck me as gentle and compassionate. He promised me he would call me as soon as Gary's body arrived. It is agonizing waiting for the body of your loved one to be brought back to you. Finally, the call came. "He's here, waiting for you."

I prepared myself to go to him quickly. I wanted to look beautiful for him. Jessi had asked me in earnest to let her go with me. She wanted to be there too. We were the only ones who wanted to be there. No one else would stand with him while his remains burned away.

Even as a little girl, I've always known that when one is being buried, they are there with those interning them. How I knew this, I don't know. How horrible would that be to appear at one's own cremation without one single loved one there? And Jessi, my sweet Jessi, understood that and wanted to be there with me and with him. I am sorry now that I did not let her. One day she will have to cremate me, and maybe it would've been easier if she'd experienced it before, let alone that I took away her right to mourn him in that way. Very rare that I made such a serious decision for her, but in this case, I thought I was sparing her more pain.

The sky was dark and threatening as it began to weep upon my windshield while I drove across Burbank Boulevard to meet him. Upon arriving at the crematorium, I first passed through a chapel-like room. Then the dear, kind gentleman, who had himself cremated hundreds, maybe thousands of bodies, led me into the oven room itself. There was a very large box on a gurney, in which lay the remains of my beloved Gary.

"Do you want to see him? He's pretty hacked up from the autopsy."

I walked up and laid my head on the box. I lifted the lid just enough to see that his chest had in fact been cracked open. Then I closed it. I placed sweetly pungent leaves and pods on top of the box. I spoke with him softly for a little while.

Then I sang to him, tears streaming down my face, "I'd give my all, to have, just one more night with you."

Then the gentle man asked, "Are you ready?"

I nodded slowly, silently.

He opened the oven door. The blast of heat was intense. He helped me roll the gurney up to be even with the door and lifted it slightly so that it could slide in smoothly. He offered to help me but I declined his assistance and pushed the box into the oven by myself, weeping. The man closed the door and cranked the flames up to maximum. I stood for a while, feeling Gary release his remains, and then I went home in the pouring rain.

A few days later I felt drawn to drive back by the house. To my great shock, one of the giant twin oaks was completely uprooted, its huge trunk and branches laying flush on the ground.

Chapter Twenty – Me

I often asked my mother in her later years, "Please let me die first." She would always respond, "Oh, don't be silly!" Then she would tenderly pat my knee or touch my shoulder. "You'll be all right." Mother always said she hoped to die in her sleep, in her own bed. I promised her she would, that I would never put her in a home.

She came to stay with us for a while after Gary left to comfort me in my mourning as much as she could and fill the gap my emotional absence was creating for Jessi. She too needed comforting, and the steady support my mother's unconditional love gave her.

I remember how, when I first found the key to my inner self, I would sit for the longest time soaking up the wonderful feeling within me. One morning I opened my eyes after an hour of turning within and everything around me was bristling with light. The sensation of my being was pulsating and divine, and I was overwhelmed with gratitude. I thought of my mother. I reached for the phone and called her. I spoke to her from where I sat, and she could hear the clarity in my voice though I could barely get the words out, I was so overcome with emotion.

"Mother, I want to thank you for carrying me for nine months, for feeding me, for clothing me, and for taking care of me until I grew up to be the happy soul I am today."

She got all choked up too. In that one moment she was totally with me, feeling what I felt, both of us saturated in bliss.

Why do we fear or dread death? I remember as a child I wondered about it a lot. Why do we die? How will I die? I tried to make bargains with God, to make a deal with him how to take me and when. I always hoped to live well past 100.

My Teacher recently pointed out a simple fact that if one lives to 70 years, that would only be 25,550 days. Even if one was fortunate enough to live to be 100, that would only be 36,500 days. It doesn't seem that long to me.

When I returned to work after Gary's death, I noticed how slowly time was passing. I was keenly aware of the seconds as they ticked off the clock. I was ultra-aware of every precious breath, knowing one day it would be gone. I felt at moments as if he was hidden only by a thin opaque veil hanging between us, that if I reached out I could touch him. I tried to understand how it was that I had lost him. I never properly questioned his hands swelling at the end of the massage as I might have, had it been anyone else. The swelling of the hands can mean many innocuous things or a heart valve problem. Then there was the counting of all the hours lost: I didn't have lunch with him that rainy day, I didn't run to him through the fierce wind when he was so sick that night. How easy it is to see what might have been when it is all over…to see the missed moments and to miss the moments we might've had.

I made up stories to get by. There was this young couple about to be married. He calls asking her to have lunch with him in the restaurant of the building where he works downtown. She tells him she is getting her nails done for the wedding. So he decides to get a hot dog at the stand across the street. A car hits him in the crosswalk and he dies. Does she ever get her nails done again?

And for my clients, who never stopped complaining about their husbands, I came up with this one:

Let's say there's this guy who makes a sandwich for himself every day, and every time he leaves the mayonnaise jar open with a knife in it on the counter. Regardless of how many times his wife asks him not to, he continues and she is sure it's just to annoy her. The day will come when she would give anything to see that open jar of mayonnaise with a knife in it left on the counter again!

***

One night when Jessi and her Grandma were already asleep, I stood in the kitchen washing dishes. As the water rinsed through my fingers, I began speaking aloud to Gary. I was angry that he left me. I was complaining about this and that, as the tears started to roll down my face, "You didn't even..."

"But I wanted to," I heard Gary say softly, as his presence was suddenly standing so close behind me.

I turned around and nearly gasped. It was him! He wrapped his arms around me ever so gently to comfort me. I gently pushed him away and walked out of the kitchen into the living room where I stood looking into the large mirror above the fireplace mantel.

Gary sat in the dining room on the mahogany captain's chair. I spoke with him at length through the mirror, and I heard his responses as tears flooded my face. He was sorry he had to leave me, we had so little time together. Yet I felt from him a deep calm, a profound peace he had now found. It was one of the most comprehensive conversations of my entire life. When we finished talking, I turned around, and there he stood wrapping me in his energy, his love, and then he was gone.

The next day my favorite forensic psychologist came to see me for a massage. I told her what had happened the night before.

She quietly commented through the face cradle of the table, "The Oracles of Delphi used mirrors to speak with the dead."

Then I understood why in Judaism when one sits shiva, the mirrors are supposed to be covered.

***

In the darkest days of my life, when I tore myself apart, at the moment before madness, I would always go within to the deepest comfort I could find, the profound peace, gently loving me and giving me the courage to go on.

My desire to flee had not yet subsided, but I needed to deal with my life from where I stood at that moment. Mother was often fond of saying, "Pull yourself up by your boot straps and carry on."

My Teacher said, "Every single human being on the face of this earth has the power to transform." And I believe it was Kabir who said, "Wake up! if you can." So I took on the task, climbed up from the graveyard of grief, and rejoined the living.

***

In 2001, Jessi was enrolled in one of the top schools for the performing arts. It was situated in the center of the Barrio, 45 minutes away from our home. It happened to be the same school Ritchie Valens attended when a plane crashed onto the schoolyard. Luckily he had not been at school that day, but the experience left him terrified of flying, turned out with good reason.

The idea of Jessi taking a bus to school was scary for me. I thought of all the things that could go wrong. But I finally had to give in and let her go. I had wrongly judged the neighborhood. All of the people in the surrounding homes helped protect the children, the school, and our cars.

Jessi auditioned for the musical theater program and got accepted. The touring group were the darlings of City Hall, famous for their excellent performances throughout Los Angeles County. The director was talented and passionate about his work and the group itself but, unfortunately, he was a power-hungry megalomaniac. He fell in love with Jessi's voice from the first time he heard her sing, so one would've thought all would go well. I took on the PR for the group and got him interviewed by CBS, so the children were seen and heard singing on the evening news.

Jessi was very good at reading people from a very early age. What she saw in the director annoyed her, and he was not able to take her kidding around, which she did a lot. The small rift that rose between them quickly became a large tear, and his response to her was extremely immature. He tried to control her, as he did everyone, hanging solos over their heads to get whatever he wanted from them. Jessi was never one to be easily manipulated. She dug her heels in and he punished her by shoving her in the back row and doing everything he could to be sure her voice would not be heard.

In eighth grade Jessi auditioned for the main show, a tribute to New York City. She sang Billy Joel's "Into the Fire" and brought the director to tears. He begrudgingly gave her that solo. She sang it with the emotion of a mature woman. How was she able to find such depth in herself? I don't know. I only know that her performance rocked everybody's world. At intermission, men and women came up to her and praised her, wiping the tears off their faces. Jessi won back the director's heart, though it settled nothing for her. On the last day of school, she went up to him, looked him straight in the eye, and said, "I'm coming back for your job." God, how I love her!

The millennium was fast approaching, the year I had always hoped to meet though never really believed I would live long enough to see. It seemed momentous to me. I asked myself, "What version of yourself will you take into the next century?" I was never taken by the Y2K madness. It was then and has always been about myself, vis-à-vis the arcs of consciousness that have been so lavishly allowed me. "Who shall I be in the face of my true self?"

Though perfection does exist and may be visited within this all too transitory form, the outward demands I placed upon myself came from a tyrannical mind. Being addicted to anything was inexcusable to me, and I was secretly ashamed of it, in particular smoking. I had tried to quit cigarettes several times. I had been successful once before with Zion's acupuncture needles, but within six months I ate my way out of my clothes and made a New Year's resolution to start smoking again. I thought of Jessi and how much I love her and how I wanted to stay alive as long as possible. I wanted to cross the millennium free of my cigarette addiction. I offered myself as a test subject for a study of how hypnosis might help one to quit smoking. I was asked to follow through with six sessions.

I informed the hypnotherapist in the first session that it was not possible to hypnotize me but that I could put myself under. He did not believe me, but I went along with the session anyway. Counting backwards 10, 9, 8... I found myself standing at the top of a palatial staircase. I started slowly down the stairs and was very surprised to find the image of Gary standing at the bottom waiting for me. I tried to understand what he was doing there. It seemed to have something to do with death.

I recalled Camus' play, The Possessed, when Stavrogin asks Kirillov, 'Everybody knows that you're going to kill yourself. Why do you work out every day?'

Kirillov answers, 'Because I want to prove that I am in my right mind, in good health, and am making this decision by myself determining my own destiny.'

For the first time I saw my addiction to cigarettes in an entirely different manner. Yes, I was wheezing, and Jessi would say that I was coughing all the time. Emphysema runs in my family. Continuing to smoke I was determining how long I would live and what I would likely die from. Looking at it from that angle I realized I had to have complete control over quitting as well. I managed to get through five sessions of hypnosis, but I never went back for the sixth.

I took a suggestion from Deepak Chopra and started counting the cigarettes with hash marks inside the top of the box. I was smoking a pack and a half a day at the most. Surprising how just taking note of the number without judgment brought the number down rather rapidly for me. I was at 11 cigarettes a day, and New Year's Eve was nearly here.

Jessi and I were invited to a party by a kind couple and their two children, who were Jessi's dear friends. I accepted the invitation with an agreement from Jessi and our hosts that she and I would be home by 10:30 pm. I've always dreaded the countdown to midnight, having spent so many years working in restaurants, standing alone while people jumped in each other's arms kissing, as if that moment meant everything. I preferred quiet reflection as the year turns, and Jessi did not seem to mind.

I was determined to quit smoking, whatever it would take, though I was afraid that I would not know myself without cigarettes. Then I remembered I had not smoked in high school, so I did remember myself before I became a smoker. By this time, society actually shunned and ostracized smokers. I once had to stand in a cage outside an Italian restaurant to have a cigarette. It was humiliating.

I decided to use the nicotine patches to help me quit. I realized that three weeks would not be enough time for me to break it off, so I would use step one for three weeks, step two for three weeks, and step three for three more. I would wear each patch for 24 hours rather than removing it at night and facing anxiety in the morning.

Jessi and I went to the charming little party for the children, who had made special cookies forming the numerals 2000. Everyone was so excited to greet the new century. At 10:15 pm we left politely as planned.

Once home, Jessi suggested we light all the candles in the house. We each scurried around gathering up as many as we could find and brought them into the living room to light. Then I lit the fireplace. The soft romantic glow of candles and firelight now illuminated the living room. Jessi beckoned me to come and rest beside her on the sofa. I put my arm around her, she laid her head gently on my shoulder, and within moments she was asleep.

I felt myself surrender totally. "I am here," I said. "I am ready." Suddenly the fireplace went out as if extinguished. Then a white, ghostlike hand, with long fingers, appeared above my head, slowly passed over the length of my body, and disappeared at my feet. My first thought was, "Who was that?" Days later, I amused myself imagining that there must've been a fight in heaven as to who was going to deliver the blessing.

In the next moment I realized it was nearly midnight, so I leapt up and went to get champagne from the fridge, popped it open, and poured a small sip for Jessi and a full glass for me in the flute glasses. I jostled Jessi slightly, and when she woke, I handed her the champagne. We toasted to the new century and sipped.

"Oooh that's warm!" Jessi said.

"That's enough!" I grabbed her glass, and we both went for the canister wands of confetti we'd purchased earlier. Jessi ran with it out the door, down the front porch, and into the yard ahead of me. I ran after her. As often happens in the most magical moments of life, every movement was in slow motion, as if I was passing through resistible air. I reached out to throw my arms around Jessi just as the confetti was flying into the air, falling ever so gently around us.

Right after we went back into the house. Jessi went straight to bed without prompting. I got in the shower, and for just a moment thought to myself, "Well, it isn't morning yet. I could have one more cigarette and quit when I get up." Then I remembered it was after midnight and I told myself, "If you ever have another cigarette, I will never let you quit again." I guess I scared myself because I did not smoke one ever again.

I struggled through the first few days like a junkie. I went to work, and when I came home, I laid down on the sofa, crunched up in fetal position, and covered myself with a blanket. I told Jessi, "Get me up ten minutes before my client comes so I can have some coffee before I try to work on them."

I made it through to the nine weeks, scared on the last day that I wouldn't be able to handle it without the patches, but I did.

Jessi took such good care of me at that time and whenever I needed her. Once when I was on my way home from work so terribly sick that I could barely drive the last 20 minutes, I called Jessi to let her know that I was coming home soon but that I was terribly ill.

"Don't worry, Mother, I'll take care of everything."

When I arrived home, I found that she had set up everything on my bed stand including water, medications, hot tea, and a boom box with the audio version of Harry Potter, as well as the books, in case I wanted her to read them to me, which I did. I was truly down for the count, and she was right there with me.

From the first day cigarette free, the wheezing I had once felt in my bronchial tubes was gone, and the coughing also gone. I remembered the hand that waved over me and I knew I had been given both the strength and the healing. Sometime later I had a lung x-ray, and to my great surprise, after all those years, there was no evident problem. I remember leaping for joy when I got the news.

Though I still smoke grass it's just not the same. Until now, many years later, I am very attracted to cigarettes and wish I could smoke one. I often stand right next to strangers who are smoking just to catch a whiff of the secondhand smoke and envy those who can smoke without care.

Jessi never knew anything about the grass until one day in the backyard when she saw a puff of smoke come out of my mouth. I tried to hide what I considered to be my faults from everyone, including her. I think I might've screamed when she saw me because she ran immediately back into the house, and I ran after her. Now I had to confess. "Jessi, it wasn't a cigarette, it's a joint."

"Oh. Okay Mom. Whew!"

My deep dark secret was out, and nothing bad happened. I hope it always works out that way.

On the anniversary of Gary's death, I got Thai food for Jessi and me, including stuffed chicken wings, and rented *The Sheltering Sky* to watch. We were both asleep long before it ended. I continued to mourn him into the next year. I spent a lot of time sleeping when I wasn't working and renting movies for Jessi and I to watch. She continued to take good care of me. I guess she must have been wondering when I would return to her. Only now do I realize how much of that time I lost, because I recall so little. Seems that all I remember from that year was quitting smoking and Jessi getting into the arts school.

When the second anniversary of his death arrived, I was convinced that only a year had passed and would continue to reference events that had actually happened in 2001 as if they occurred in 2000, until just recently, when I finally realized that I had lost a year altogether. I still miss him, as I always will.

My Teacher was holding a weeklong event in Australia. It was a yearly retreat that I had always wanted to attend. But I was worried about Jessi. I was the only one she had to care for her, except for Grandma, who was aging all too quickly. I wrestled with the idea for some time. I even went so far as to buy the tickets and register for the event.

Mother was already there with us, having agreed to stay with Jessi. My packed bags were standing in a heap on the bedroom floor. As the moment to leave drew closer, I became more and more disoriented. I could not let go of the feeling that it was not fair to Jessi to take even the slightest chance, be it one in a million, that I would not be able to come back and finish raising her. I stumbled around, torn between my desire to go and my love for my precious daughter. By then Jessi was asking me, "Mother please, just sit down a minute." She wasn't trying to keep me from going; she just wanted to stop the mania. I was buzzing around like a fly, unable to find an open window. When I finally tripped over my suitcases and fell on the floor, I realized there was no question; I was staying home. I understood my responsibility was to my daughter.

After a deep sigh I decided to turn what seemed like a disaster into fun for all of us. I remembered seeing these little cabins up Temescal Canyon that reminded me of where Snow White might have lived, complete with all the surrounding nature and a babbling brook. I thought it would be wonderful to stay together there. So I rented us a cabin with bunkbeds that was large enough to hold six people. We were, in fact, the only people staying there aside from the very few neighbors who lived there. Mother and Jessi both agreed to come and were quite pleased when we arrived. I brought with me everything we could possibly need for snacks including my espresso machine to steam milk for hot cocoa.

After we had settled in, Mother announced she'd like to take a nap. I gave her a bed by the open window, where she could hear the brook rushing over the rocks and the frogs croaking right alongside our cabin. Jessi and I headed up the mountain for a hike. I'm sorry to say I don't recall ever having hiked with her before or since, but we had a wonderful time. We hiked for an hour and a half up to the waterfall and back, all without me wheezing or becoming short of breath. I know my way around paths and what to watch out for since I spent my childhood wandering through the forest, having been a Girl Scout. I am glad that I had the chance to share that with Jessi, and I believe she had fun too.

When we returned to the cabin, Mother was just waking. She seemed to be really enjoying herself. It must have been a long time since she had been surrounded by nature like this. Jessi and I washed up, getting ready to drive down the canyon for a sumptuous dinner at a restaurant by the sea. When we arrived, the hostess informed us it would be an hour and a half wait. I knew Mother could not cope with that long a wait, even if she could sit down. So I took the young lady aside and told her, "My mother is disabled. She cannot stand for an hour and a half. I need a booth by the window, now!"

I might not have been quite that rude about it, but we were seated in five minutes where Mother could see the sunset and watch the sea. A school of dolphins went leaping by. Mother was delighted. She had never seen them before, and I was so pleased to see the childlike glee on her face!

Dinner was absolutely delicious, and we ate to our hearts' content. Then on our way back up to the cabin, a deer came out to greet us. Evidently, Mother had never seen a deer in their natural habitat either. It made her night. In the morning we hung out as long as we could, then headed home through the Palisades, stopping for a little lunch along the way, two very beautiful days.

When Mother's Day came, I took Jessi with me to Miami while I attended an event with my Teacher. I invited my mother to come as well, but Joseph, who at that time was still alive and living with her, had asked that she stay with him that day. She explained to me that he had never requested to spend Mother's Day with her and she was not inclined to refuse him. I accepted her decision with quiet reluctance, not arguing to change her mind. I too was a mother now and I understood. I kept in touch with my dear mother throughout that weekend and though there were no special plans, Joseph had her with him, and that was enough. Now I can see the simple beauty of it. He was her last born and would always be her baby. Mother was concerned what would become of him when she died. So she left the house to Joseph in her will and made my oldest brother the trustee. I remember him insisting he didn't want to be, realizing that it would make him Joseph's guardian.

Of course I wanted Jessi to find peace within, inside herself one day, but I have always felt that it is a highly individual search. The best I could do was continue my efforts to live in that peace myself and hope she would be inspired to find it for herself. I have to admit, I could have done better. Bringing Jessi with me was not at all about indoctrination. It was really about taking her to Miami for the first time and letting her enjoy that. I think it was the last time that arrangements had been made for mothers who wanted to attend an event and were in need of childcare. Children under the age of eight were not allowed to attend, and only those who wanted to attend out of their own interest were encouraged.

I was glad to be taking Jessi to my favorite hotel on the beach in Miami, now called the Wyndham. It had all the elegance of the Fontainebleau on a slightly smaller scale, including a luxurious pool right on the beach before the cabanas and the warm sea. The moment we crossed over the bridge to Collins Avenue, Jessi said, "I love it here!" It was so much fun to please her. We had plenty of time to spend long hours hanging out by the pool when I wasn't attending the events, which generally speaking, only lasted about two hours. In the evenings we would go to an excellent restaurant.

There was one unfortunate consequence to our many otherwise enjoyable hours in the sun. Early on, I called Jessi over to me and suggested she put sunscreen on. She declined insisting, "Our skin types are different, Mother. I don't burn the way you do!"

I stupidly let her go thinking, "Okay, maybe she's right. She does have that Adani blood, so maybe she doesn't burn in the sun." She wound up getting on the plane with one of the worst sunburns I've ever seen, so painful it was even difficult for her to sit. When we got home, I poured milk all over her as she stood in the bathtub, then Aloe Vera, gave her aspirin, and she was off to bed. It was totally due to my negligence, imagining that she could make all her own decisions simply because she insisted.

In the summer that followed, Mother was struggling desperately trying to deal with the pain of bone-on-bone arthritis in her knees. The vicodin made her skin itch, and the dermagesic patches filled with morphine made her feel sick and woozy. I was hell on wheels dealing with her Medicare HMO. The phone calls alone with the wait times were laborious, far too difficult for someone of Mother's age to deal with. The insurance companies make it so difficult for an old person to ever get through that they just give up. I navigated the system and forced the HMO to use every resource possible to help get her out of pain. I insisted that she only be seen by the best in the field of pain management. She was finally given an appointment with an excellent doctor equipped to do a difficult spinal injection to help with the pain. His office was in Pasadena, Mother lived in San Dimas, and I lived in Encino. So that meant I would have to drive to San Dimas to get her, take her to Pasadena, then take her back home again, and drive back to Encino, all in all a journey of over 100 miles. Sadly, nothing is made convenient even when one does work their way through the system. She opted to stay with us for a few days after the injection to see how it went. Though she got some relief, unfortunately, it disappeared quickly.

We had been told years before that a knee replacement was in order for both knees. Nadera had told me it was a relatively easy procedure these days. Mother was just at the border of an age where such an operation would not be too difficult to recover from. Then I considered the remote possibility that she could die during the surgery and selfishly did not encourage her to have it. God, how I wish I had. Instead I complained to her over the phone one day about the difficulty of managing her medical affairs and the hours I had to spend on the phone talking with the HMO.

Suddenly, I could hear her weeping, "Do you mean you're not going to help me anymore?"

"Oh no, Mother, I am so sorry. Of course, I am going to keep helping you. I love you. I will not abandon you!" We both cried.

The summer was coming to an end, and it was time to plan Jessi's 12th birthday party. I figured this time I wanted to try a surprise party. So I made arrangements for a group of 20 at a local restaurant and went early to set up the banquet table, decorating it in a Harry Potter theme. Then I went back home to bring Jessi and Grandma to the waiting party. It does seem unlikely that Jessi was entirely surprised, but she didn't seem completely pleased either. How did I not know she hates surprises?

My mother had very kindly decided to come despite the fact that she was having what would turn out to be a paradoxical reaction to the prednisone she had just been prescribed over the phone by a doctor who hadn't seen her in two years, and who, having no idea what she weighed, gave her a dosage strong enough for a 250-pound man. I knew nothing of Mother's call to that doctor until the medication was already in complication mode. She appeared to be on a high similar to that of cocaine, manifesting symptoms of insatiable thirst and a constant craving for candy. She had hardly slept in days. I called the doctor who had given her the prescription, screaming. She said that she could just stop taking the prednisone without titrating it down and prescribed a heavy tranquilizer in its place.

Jessi and I were sitting in the living room when we heard a thud in the bedroom. It was Grandma, having fallen face down on the floor. It was very lucky she didn't break her nose, though it was black and blue. She took it all so cheerfully, for Jessi's sake, I believe.

"Oh, don't worry about me. I'll be all right." She was clearly unstable from the medication, and here again the seriousness of the situation was escaping me.

The day after Jessi's party I insisted we go shopping at Macy's, pushing my mother around in a wheelchair. A passerby took one look at her sitting hunched over, appearing to be great distress, then looked at me as if I was crazy. Again, it seems I was blind.

I had promised to take Mother home the next day but as we pulled onto the freeway Jessi started crying. I had already asked my mother to stay longer and when she asked Jessi why she was crying she said, "Because, I'm afraid I will never see you again."

I turned again to my mother and said, "Mother please, I cannot take you home like this!"

"Okay."

She agreed to stay. I pulled off the freeway, and we went back home. Jessi spent much of the afternoon singing songs for Grandma that she would sing at school in the upcoming year.

The following day we took her home but I did not let her take the tranquilizers with her. Kate had suggested it would be too dangerous for her to be falling all around her house. Mother was furious with me for keeping her pills.

"I don't know what will happen to me tonight!"

Joseph's answer was to put a morphine patch on to calm her down. It was a Tuesday. Jessi and I were standing together waiting for service in a Sprint store when I got the call. It was Joseph.

"Mom's dead." He hung up.

I told Jessi. She burst into tears. Then after a few moments she stopped crying, turned to me and said, "Grandma's gone on vacation…permanently."

I don't recall seeing her cry again over Grandma, not because of a lack of caring or loving her. It was something she understood or at least accepted.

I was quickly inconsolable. I had to call Kate to get the details my brother Bill had given her. Joseph found Mother dead that morning. She had died in her sleep, in her own bed, during the night. When I knew where her body had been taken, I called the mortuary to let them know I was on my way to see her. I was told that they would close at 5 o'clock.

"I'm an hour away from there but I should make it by five. Please wait for me even if I am a little late."

Just as we were approaching the mortuary about to turn into the parking lot, Jessi started shaking her finger at me insistently demanding in a raised voice, "I don't want you to blame anyone for this! Do you understand me?"

I was alarmed by Mother's presence manifesting for a moment through my daughter. But I heard her loud and clear, and I would have to obey.

We were standing at the mortuary doors, already locked. There was no answer to my repeated knocks. I started screaming and pounding on the doors frantically demanding that they come and open them.

"Yes, I know someone is in there. Open these doors! You promised to wait for me!"

I walked around the building banging on every window, still no response. Though I knew there were more than dead bodies in there, none were kind enough to respond. Jessi tried futilely to calm me down. My sweet mother's remains lay inside. How could I kiss her? How could I hold her now? I cried out for her and continued ranting until a cop arrived, luckily an Irish one. I explained that I wanted to see my mother's body.

He seemed to understand my grief, saying, "Just go peacefully and come back tomorrow when they open."

It was with Mother's death that I saw when God wants to take your loved one, he hoodwinks you, grabs them, and then whips the bag off your head!

We went from the mortuary to Grandma's house. I think I was expecting to find Joseph there, but he was not. Suspecting that it would be my last chance ever to stand in my mother's home, now that it was Joseph's, I took a few of her things with me for Jessi and Kate's daughter, and a beaded Christmas sweater for myself. Then I went into the dining room, and as quickly and carefully as I possibly could, wrapped every piece of her wedding crystal that she had promised to me and walked out of her house for the last time. I wish now I had taken everything or at least much more, because in the end my brothers would sell what they could and throw the rest of her precious belongings in the trash.

I had told my mother that I put a codicil on my life insurance policy affording my brothers $100,000 to split should Jessi and I pre-decease them. Joseph got it into his head that I had taken out a $100,000 insurance policy on my mother's life and was refusing to share it with them. Not one of them even tried to get the facts straight. They didn't speak to me for the next five years, leaving Jessi without uncles. Each of them would one day come back, asking for forgiveness in their own way, and I gave it to them.

Kate told me she was coming to the funeral only for me. She was concerned how my brothers might behave in that they were all drunks. Two of my dearest friends also flew to my side: Irene, who diligently put together a collage of Mother's photos, and Julie, who helped with the production that the memorial reception would be. I used the large Community Recreation Room at the mobile Estates Village where she lived and invited all of her friends there, as well as family. I ordered all of her favorite dishes from various restaurants around town including chicken wings. I made large quantities of her fabulous potato salad and her delicious macaroni and shrimp salad, so it would be as if she'd made it for everyone herself. Then I ordered two large decorated cakes, as if it was her birthday, all to celebrate her life with a fine feast.

One of her dearest friends, who was quite fond of Joseph but never thought much of me, would tell me point blank that it was my fault Mother was dead. I knew well enough the truth and did not take it to heart, but it is incredible how cruel people can be.

Jessi attended the Rosary held on the night before Mother's burial, which was Jessi's first day of 7th grade. I realized that missing the first day of school to attend her grandmother's funeral and then having to go back on the second day to explain why she hadn't been there and relive the entire day all over, was not what Grandma would've wanted for her. As if inspired by my mother, I talked it over with Jessi, and we both decided it would be best for her to skip the funeral and go to school. Joseph was not able to attend at all. I am sure none of us could've known the depth of his heartache. Mother was his whole world.

Kate and I went together to the church. I gave an impromptu eulogy after my oldest brother struggled through his. At the end, I explained that there was a song in Hebrew, "the language of Christ," I said, turning momentarily to the priest, that I had always promised Mother I would sing at her funeral and that I would like to sing for them all now. First, I translated the simple verse for them. I believe it is Shimi Tavori's song. "Ema, at ani ohevite. Mother, I love you. Ema, toda m'cole ha levite, Mother, thank you with all my heart, toda m'cole ha levite, Ema! Thank you with all my heart, Mother!"

Then I sang it with every pore of my being, my voice thundering through the walls and ceiling of the church. Kate said later that she wanted to stand up and cheer.

The following Tuesday was 9/11. It was nearly 6 am. Jessi was up watching TV while she blow-dried her hair before school, when suddenly she cried out from her bedroom, "Mom, come quick!"

I was by her side in seconds.

"Look at this!"

"My God, what happened?"

"They're saying the pilot purposely flew the plane into the building!"

"No," I remarked in disbelief, barely audible.

Just then the phone rang. I ran into the kitchen to get it. It was Simon, asking if we were okay, explaining that it was already on TV in Israel. Then Jessi suddenly screamed in terror. I hung up the phone and ran to her. She saw the second plane hit the other building.

"Oh my God, honey!" I wrapped my arms around her and held her for a moment. I now know they planned it that way. There would be a little lag time after the first plane hit so the cameras would be watching when the second plane hit and everyone would see it happen.

I told Jessi she could stay home, but she wanted to go to school. I drove her there myself. Had I known her teachers would play the news all day long, I would never have taken her.

I called Kate on my way to work. She warned me, "Don't let yourself be hurt by this. That's what they want, to bring fear and darkness. Stand in the light where it cannot touch you."

As I stood in my darkened room, beginning to work on the first client of the day, I had a vision of them and their leader, toasting each other with sweetened mint tea and brandy, in the shadows of a fire-lit cave. I promised myself I would never speak any of their names again.

Soon after, a former client came looking for me at the reception desk of the spa. She wasn't there for a massage. She wanted to ask me something that she needed to hear from me. I was called to the desk to find her leaning over the counter in earnest, her dark eyes looking deep into mine for an answer. "Is it going to be all right?"

I held her a moment in my glance. "Yes!"

She took a deep sigh of relief, turned, and went about her day.

Tuesday, two weeks ago, my mother died. Last Tuesday was 9/11. This Tuesday, today, was Rosh Hashanah and my birthday. Jessi was at school, and I was taking the day off. It was still early morning. I took my grandmother's pink brocade bed cover and went to sit on the overstuffed armchair by the fireplace in the living room. I covered myself with the lovely spread.

Then suddenly came the presence of my mother, with my father in hand. I could feel them standing together near me. It was as if Mother had brought him to see me. I felt their love so profoundly and that they were proud of me. I told them I loved them too and thanked them. It was one of the most touching moments of my life and then they left me, softly.

As I went inside to my true self, a thought struck me that while the world was at war, I sat sheltered by the mantle of Love, floating in a harbor of Peace.

All I had ever longed for was always there, waiting. Joy is just a step away from misery. It is said that one can experience this peace even on a battlefield. I feel the lift of wings long denied and I begin to soar.

Chapter Twenty-One – Epilogue

Years later, I find myself sitting on the beach. The water sparkles, lit by the setting sun that will dissolve all too quickly when it touches the horizon.

In the background, I hear the laughter of my friends, sipping their drinks as they mingle together, enjoying the view of the sea that borders our beautiful home from one end to the other. The party I prepared for them is in full swing and my kind, charming partner is chatting with some of our dearest while grilling in the backyard.

I've briefly ducked away, as I sometimes do, taking a moment for myself before returning to the celebration. We just got back from South America and we'll be leaving for another tour of Europe soon, so I savor these quiet moments whenever I can. The breeze softly sweeps across my face. I take a deep breath as my head tilts scanning the sky. I remember everything—the triumphs and the tragedies, the joy and the misery, the foolishness and the miracles—and still the ocean roars.

Acknowledgements

I am Grateful…

To John F. Quinlan and Jeanette Blanche (Witkowski) Quinlan, my parents, for their love and individual roles in shaping my character.

To Ora Cummings, my agent, for her enthusiasm, kindness, excellent editing and genuine friendship.

To Ian Hooper, my publisher, for reading it, loving it, and giving it a chance.

To Sherry Weinstein for her watchful eye, considered comments and loving inspiration.

To Mark William Spradley, for his steadfast honesty and unwavering loyalty.

To Steven Whitney, for his professional advice and his extraordinary generosity.

To Kathleen Mary Quinlan, for her constant love and guidance.

To Raphael "Ella" Quinlan, my daughter, for all she has taught me about compassion, tolerance and Love.

And finally, to Timothy Gallwey, my loving husband, for all that he is to me, my lover, my protector, and of course, my coach!

About the Author

Barbara Ann Quinlan was born in upstate New York and later raised in Southern California. For six years, she studied a radical form of eastern European theater; first with Leonidas Dudarew-Ossentynski at his studio in Hollywood and then at the Theater Laboratory of Jerzy Grotowski, in Wrocław, Poland.

Her studies included No and Kabuki Theater, ancient Chinese resonator techniques for the voice, Thai Chi and Chi gung, among countless other exercises aimed at breaking down one's resistances in order to develop the actor as a superhuman; capable of performing far beyond the normal human range.

Barbara wrote her first poem at five and has kept numerous journals. She studied French in Paris, Spanish in school and Hebrew in Israel. Throughout the years, she has used her knowledge of Chi gung to perform energetic healing.

After spending ten years traveling as the executive assistant to a well-known author who gives seminars around the world, Barbara now dedicates herself to the joys of life itself, her family, her friends and her writing.

www.ingramcontent.com/pod-product-compliance
Lightning Source LLC
Chambersburg PA
CBHW020321010526
44107CB00054B/1932